A good speech is a powerful implement. A great speech can turn the course of history. But if there is one thing that strikes fear into the hearts of many people, it is the thought of public speaking. Even the most experienced presenter can get it wrong. Yet in this media-dominated world, it is something that no one with any ambition can easily avoid. It's as simple as this: Good communicators have better careers.

People remember stories, not facts. *StoryWorks* demonstrates the sheer power of storytelling. The power to influence and persuade. The power to sell or change a point of view. *StoryWorks* is an invaluable handbook which will help you master a few simple techniques and become an impactful speaker whether you are addressing two or three people, or two or three hundred. **Jeff Grout**, Business Speaker & Executive Consultant, Listed in the '100 Best Business Speakers in Britain'

Telling a good tale is key to holding an audience's attention. A gifted storyteller herself, Jane Bain's show-and-tell method of teaching goes down as easily as a bowl of Goldilocks' 'just-right' porridge. Her five-finger technique demystifies narrative for those who want their stories to grab readers and listeners like Bain's do.
Susan Welsh, Book Reviewer & Journalist

Storytelling is an essential part of selling yourself. Whether you're applying for a new job, pitching for an internal promotion or networking with colleagues, other people's perception of who you are and what you're good at is shaped by your ability to tell your story. However, many people struggle to tell their story effectively.

Interview questions such as, "Tell me about yourself?" are commonly used and often the most challenging to answer. *StoryWorks* is one of the most useful handbooks I have seen for anyone looking to improve workplace performance and career prospects. An awful lot of career success is built around perception rather than fact: storytelling is the new marketing!
Tony Heard, CEO, Abintegro Career Management

We all have a story in us. *StoryWorks* tells you how to get it out. This book explores why we tell stories and how they can help us relay information in a more interesting way. Written in a clear, accessible style for anyone who wants no-nonsense practical advice on how to tell stories.
Susie Lynes, Writing Coach

StoryWorks

A Handbook for Leaders,
Writers and Speakers

StoryWorks

A Handbook for Leaders,
Writers and Speakers

Jane Bailey Bain

**BUSINESS
BOOKS**

Winchester, UK
Washington, USA

First published by Business Books, 2015
Business Books is an imprint of John Hunt Publishing Ltd., Laurel House, Station Approach,
Alresford, Hants, SO24 9JH, UK
office1@jhpbooks.net
www.johnhuntpublishing.com

For distributor details and how to order please visit the 'Ordering' section on our website.

ISBN: 978 1 78279 986 3
Library of Congress Control Number: 2014958363

A CIP catalogue record for this book is available from the British Library.

Design: Stuart Davies

Printed and bound by CPI Group (UK) Ltd, Croydon, CR0 4YY, UK

We operate a distinctive and ethical publishing philosophy in all
areas of our business, from our global network of authors to
production and worldwide distribution.

CONTENTS

For Kyrian, Wulfie & Annapurna
who have listened to all my stories.

Part I: The Power Of Story

People who can use words well are powerful. There is an old saying that the pen is mightier than the sword. Humans are toolmakers, and words are the greatest tool known to mankind. Sticks and stones may bruise you, but words can touch your mind and heart. And words are strongest when they are woven together into stories.

Anyone who works with words knows the power of story. The tales you hear help you to understand things that have happened to you. The tales you tell influence how other people see you. You use stories to make sense of the world.

Inspirational leaders and public speakers understand and use the force of narrative.
Top trainers and therapists know that stories are a tool for personal transformation.
Great writers and storytellers know that words have the power to shape reality.

This book will help you to tell stories more effectively. Whether you're a business manager who needs to motivate your staff, a teacher trying to get your point across or a writer looking for inspiration, you'll find techniques here to inform, to instruct and to entertain.

Tell Me A Story

YOU are a natural born storyteller. Every day you make up stories and tell them to your friends. You use stories to tell people about yourself and to inform them about the world. Sometimes you tell a tale just to make someone laugh. Many of your stories are unique and personal. They are based on things you have seen or heard, and events you have experienced. By choosing what to include in your tale, you decide what is important. You take real things that happen in your life and weave them into a meaningful sequence of events.

When two people get together, they start to tell stories. Friends meeting in a cafe. Colleagues back at work on Monday morning. Strangers sitting together on a long-distance bus. We meet and we say, Tell me your story.
"How are you?"
"How was your weekend?"
"How is your journey going?"
"Fine" simply doesn't answer the question.

Humans are storytelling animals. Other creatures communicate in different ways – the honeybee's waggle, the dog's warning bark – but only human beings string words together to form meaningful narratives of events. We use stories to explain, to teach and to entertain. When you want people to remember something, a good story makes it memorable. If you have to give an unwelcome message, a clever story renders it more palatable. And when you just want to amuse an audience, there's nothing better than a well-told tale.

Why do we tell stories? Because they are the most effective form of communication. Stories work in many different ways. On the surface, they provide a narrative sequence of events. When one thing leads to another, we assume that the first incident caused the second. This is reassuring: it gives us a sense of meaning and purpose in life. At a deeper level, they speak to us with parallels and similes. They communicate both overt messages and implied meanings. Most of all, stories harness the power of imagery to work their magic on our minds.

Imagery is an incredibly powerful tool both for persuasion and for personal development. Everything that has ever been made – from an omelette to a space rocket – began as a picture in someone's mind. Images provide a representation that can be transformed into a real thing. They provide us with a focus for our thoughts and efforts. And they let us image-ine how things could be different: a metaphor provides the basis for metamorphosis.

When you meet other people, you communicate with them by telling stories. You recall a series of events and you string them together into a causal narrative sequence. In other words, you turn your own experiences into a story. You also listen to other people's narratives. Their anecdotes show you how they have dealt with similar situations. Stories help you to interpret things that have happened to you. They provide possible templates for future action. A good story touches both your mind and your heart. Hearing stories can shift your perceptions and shape your dreams. Telling tales creates new possibilities in your mind.

In The Beginning

Since ancient times, the person who could tell stories has been admired and respected. Our ancestors understood the deep power of stories. When someone wanted to boast, they told tales of their hunting prowess. When they wanted to honour another, they turned their deeds into epic sagas. When they wanted to warn against misbehaviour, they related parables and fables. Myths and legends provided social commentary and recorded earliest history. Wordweavers held the heritage of their people in trust.

For a long time, the only way that tales could be transmitted was by repetition. In hunting tribes, the deepest wisdom was the province of specialists who we might now call shamans or medicine men. Wise elders would use stories to explain the world and pass on practical information. Gradually humankind learnt farming skills and settled communities were established. The agricultural surplus they produced could support an elite class of rulers. Priests were entrusted with sacred stories which were retold with ceremonial ritual. Bards and troubadours travelled between villages carrying news and spreading songs. Folktales survived because women told them to entertain children.

Over five thousand years ago, systems of symbols were developed which allowed sacred stories to be recorded. The earliest forms of writing emerged in the great Bronze Age civilizations of the Middle East. Methods such as Sumerian cuneiform and Egyptian hieroglyph were cumbersome, requiring scribes to memorize hundreds of word-symbols. By 1150 BC the Phoenicians were using a phonetic alphabet of 22 consonant letters. The Greeks adopted this around 750 BC and added vowel sounds. This system forms the basis of all Western alphabets. It is simple to learn and easy to read. Finally writing had become accessible to anyone who cared to learn.

The first scholars were a privileged group. Only the wealthy and the clergy could afford to sit around reading and writing manuscripts. It was not until the invention of the printing press that books became widely available. The mass production of books in Renaissance Europe changed the whole structure of society. No longer did people have to rely on wandering minstrels and town criers for news. Information could be acquired – or disseminated – by anyone with an interest. By the nineteenth century, industrial presses were in widespread use. From Bibles to political manifestos, from novels to instruction manuals, the world was flooded with printed matter. Two hundred years later, computer technology added to this verbal inundation.

People have become cynical about the printed word: 'You can't believe everything you read.' Yet we still depend mainly on words for communication. As a speaker or writer, you're part of a venerable tradition. Words have the power to persuade, to teach, and to entertain. This last function is perhaps the most important. Words work best when they are woven into stories. The craft of the storyteller is to spin a thread of narrative. Whether the stories are presented to an audience, or written down in a novel, or related to spellbound children, the wordsmith must first weave a meaningful series of events.

Making Meaning

Stories are far more than just light entertainment. You use them to make sense of your life. We visit fictional worlds because they shed light on our own reality. A tale well told should be both beautiful and functional. Stories enrich our lives and nourish our spirits. They provide a framework for understanding what has happened to us. They give a model for how we could or should behave. The heart does not distinguish between fiction and biography. Both show us how other people have responded to similar situations; they reassure us that we too will survive. In this sense, stories are the language of the soul.

Let's start close to home. The most important story in your life is your own story. You use narrative to make sense of the world around you. When you think about your life, you are constantly formulating a set of questions:

What happened on that day?
When exactly was that?
Whereabouts was I?
Who else was involved?
Why did it happen? Why me?
How has that affected my life since?

Your answers to these questions determine how you see yourself. The explanations you give publicly affect how other people see you. What has happened to you before, and how you see it, has a strong influence on what will happen to you next. As you interpret your past, you are unconsciously developing expectations for the future. These predictions tend to come true, as your expectations influence what you see in the world. Your answers to the questions above lead to self-fulfilling prophecies. You modify your own personal story in the light of what has happened, and this affects what you expect to happen next. In this way, you are constantly developing your own life script.

The stories that you hear affect the way you see the world. Your internal 'library' of tales is determined by many factors. The most influential stories are probably those which you heard as a child. *Cinderella; Jack GiantKiller; Beauty and the Beast* – these are the figures which informed you in childhood and accompanied you into adult life. They provided role models for your own behaviour and a way of interpreting the people you encounter. Although they are often dismissed as fairytales, these stories formed the first material for you to interpret the world.

As you grew older, these classic tales were supplemented by other sources of narrative. Books, films and plays gave you other ideas for possible roles. Newspapers and magazines portray different ways of being and behaving. They might appear new, but closer analysis reveals that the characters from your childhood recur in these more adult narratives. They may wear different guises, but the hero is still being heroic; the good mother is still supportive; the ogre still lurks outside the door. This is because they are based on universally recurring figures called 'archetypes', which are discussed later on.

You still use stories to make sense of the world. You weave a narrative which helps you to understand your life experiences. This life script is selectively edited in line with your self-image. You tell anecdotes to inform other people about yourself. These tales form the basis of your public persona. You use stories to explain and justify and persuade. They are an inextricable part of your life, because telling stories is what makes us human.

It's Not Personal

Maybe you like hearing stories, but you don't think you have a tale to tell. Think again: we all use stories in everyday life. When you chat over the dinner table, you talk about what happened to you today. When you text a friend, you give them updates about what's happening. When you write a report, you start by saying why it was commissioned. When you go to the doctor, you tell them the history of your symptoms. The best speeches at weddings and funerals are full of personal anecdotes. And obituaries are interesting because they tell the story of someone's life.

You can't beat a good story. Telling tales is simply the best way to get your point across. A story can convey a message, or provide a warning, or create a sense of identity. Books portray a particular world view; plays often have a political agenda. Influential leaders use narrative to inspire their followers. Priests deliver sermons that refer to scriptural stories. Politicians use anecdotes to sway public opinion. Lawyers convince a jury with their interpretation of events. Newspaper editors say that facts tell, but stories sell. That's why the best journalists are good storytellers.

Stories are the best way of selling something too. What you're trying to sell could be a product, or a policy, or just your personal services. You can quote statistics until you're blue in the face but most people respond better to words than numbers. Speakers become more interesting when they are telling a real-life story. Presentations are more effective when they include some personal anecdotes. This is because stories evoke our sympathy, an insight that can be put to good use.

Let's look at some examples of how stories work better than plain facts.

'In Tiruna, less than 15% of the population can read. Only 1 child in 5 attends school, and of these only 1/10 continue their education after the third grade. Female literacy levels are half the national average, with implications for maternal health and childcare.'

"This is Ima. She is twelve years old and she wants to be a doctor. Ima goes to school in her village, but her family can't afford to buy pens or books. For just ten pounds you can provide the things which Ima so desperately needs."

Which gets you to put your hand in your pocket?

'Statistical analysis shows that around 1% of household electrical appliances will suffer a serious electrical fault at some point. Not all insurance policies provide for this type of eventuality.'

"Have you heard? Penny Wilmot's dishwasher blew up in the night. No-one was hurt, but the kitchen is ruined. She's moving in with her mother-in-law for three months while they renovate. Thank goodness the insurance covered it."

Which makes you go home and check the small print on your own policy?

'Drugs are very dangerous. Around 2% of users are seriously affected the first time they try illegal substances. For this reason, convictions for dealing in class A drugs carry a lengthy prison sentence.'

"My name's Nat. I'm a lot tougher than you'll ever be. I've been on the streets. Made my stash. Drugs is easy money, see? But I don't do that no more. It's not worth it. I'm here to tell you about life on the inside."

Which talk gets the teenage boys' attention?

Whatever you're offering, you're much more likely to reach your audience if you can offer them an engaging tale.

Maybe you don't have a product to sell? You're still in the business of pitching your script. You want a new job? A strong application depends on a good CV. And your curriculum vitae is literally your life story. You want to go on a date? Your chances are largely due to how you present yourself. You go to a school reunion? Everyone is busy talking about what they've been up to in the intervening years. Even getting on with the neighbours depends on how you sell your story. Are you a good guy who gives sympathy and support, or an old grump who gets no worse than he deserves? Like it or loathe it, you define yourself by your script. People are narrative junkies: we all respond to a good story.

Tips Of The Trade

Wordworking is a skilled craft. In traditional societies, the person who could tell a good story has always been admired. Whether you are delivering a speech, selling a pitch, chatting with friends or writing a book, you should be able to tell a good tale.

Everyone should know a few stories. Not memorized by heart, but rather the way a jazz musician knows a piece of music: you know the major chords so that you can improvise around them. You can adapt your basic repertoire of stories to suit your audience. (Warning: Children love to hear the same story told over and over again and will correct the smallest variation!) Speakers, writers and storytellers can use their favourite tales like basic recipe ingredients, blending them and adding different details to create a new dish. There are a few professional tricks which can help improve your work. So here are the things to consider when telling your story.

Beginning, Middle, End

Let's begin by studying the structure of a simple storytelling session. The basic laws of narration apply whether you are addressing a small group or a large meeting. The same principles of structure apply for writers too. You'll see in the next section how you can expand this three-step model to novels and scripts.

When you are telling a story, remember to start at the beginning and finish at the end. It sounds simple, but you would be surprised how often people forget this basic rule. One old adage is to 'tell the audience what you're going to tell them about; tell them; and tell them you've told them'. That way, there can be no doubt about the point or conclusion of your talk.

"I'm going to tell you a story about a girl who was afraid of the dark."

When you tell a story, you create an imaginary world. You must start by setting the scene. Choose a point in time, or state of affairs, that are relevant either to your story or to the audience.

"Gill had always hated her sister."

"Do you all live around here? Gill came from this town too..."

So your story must start at the beginning. Not too early, and certainly not too late. Do we really need to know about the heroine's childhood? Maybe yes: she was a foundling and never felt that she belonged; the bad fairy was not invited to her christening. Maybe not: one of her school teachers was mean to her. That might be important to you, but unless it will be meaningful to other people, then keep it secret. Your audience don't have to know everything about your characters. In fact, authors often know lots of things about their characters that they never tell anyone. It helps them to round out their personalities and make their actions more believable.

But it is equally important to begin at a point which is early enough to set the scene properly. You don't want to start so late that you need to keep adding extra information. Flashbacks can work, but they need to be planned. You shouldn't suddenly say, "It was particularly upsetting for Elaine because she had been bullied as a child." That makes it hard for the reader to follow your story. If you are writing a novel, you might decide to have a moment when the protagonist remembers an earlier incident. If you're telling an anecdote, that just shows you haven't planned it properly.

The main part of your story is the middle. If you're composing a story, a good way of planning it is the 'story mountain'. Take a piece of paper and draw a mountain: a line going up then down. Then plot your narrative as a journey over this mountain. You start on the bottom left side by describing how things are when your story begins. This sets the scene for future action. Then something happens to change this state of affairs. Your hero/ine responds to this incident, and their life will never be the same again. You gradually build up tension with dramatic events. Write these out as steps going up the mountain: three steps overall is a good manageable number. (See the Rule of Threes section later on.) Eventually you reach the dramatic climax, the event which decides the outcome of your story. On your story plan, note down this scene at the top of your mountain. Then you quickly slide down to reach the bottom on the other side: the outcome of the story. Everything is normal again, but the crucial point is different: the monster has been slain; the prize has been won.

Your story mountain will look something like this:

```
                            Crucial  Hero's
                            climax   re-action
                    Dramatic  Hero's
                    event     action
        New    Hero's                         Resolution
        factor response
Initial                                       Outcome
scene                                          (Sequel)
```

The ending of your story is important. You want to tie up everything and account for important characters: don't leave a lone vampire assassin on the loose. If you have a message or a moral, decide whether you want to spell it out. Sometimes it is more effective if you leave the audience to draw their own conclusions.

Plan the last line of your story carefully: this is the final impression that your story will make. Usually you will have decided the ending in advance – although sometimes events may surprise you. Fictional characters have a habit of taking on lives of their own! If you find yourself relating how the dragon set up house with the princess, go along with your instincts. This sort of ad-libbing is often a response to the mood of a live audience. If you are sensitive to your listeners, you will be a better storyteller. Whatever happens, the mood of your ending should match the tone of your story. At this point, don't try to go for clever twists or surprise outcomes. You want people to feel satisfied that everything has been properly wrapped up.

"So Gill was never scared of the dark wood again."
Unless of course you're planning a sequel...

Studying Structure

We've talked about building your 'story mountain'. You identify three 'steps' or major events which form the basis for your narrative. If you're making a business point or telling a training tale, you can use this basic model to plan your speech. For public speakers, the dramatic incline should be steep. You have to grab the audience's attention fast, and hold it tightly. Anecdotes must be tailored to the specific needs of your listeners. For other types of narrative, you can adapt the same technique. Let's see how the three-stage model applies to the world's best-known story.

Cinderella (Classic fairytale)
Initial scene: Cinders sits in the kitchen, dressed in rags.
Step 1. New factor: Her fairy godmother appears and transforms her.
Heroine's response: Cinderella goes off to the Royal Ball.
Step 2. Dramatic event: The Prince sees her and they dance together all night.

Heroine's action: Cinderella leaves at midnight, but she drops her slipper.

Step 3. Crucial climax: The prince picks up the glass slipper and searches for her.

Heroic re-action: Cinderella comes out of the kitchen and tries on the slipper.

Resolution: The glass slipper fits perfectly.

Outcome: The prince marries her.

Fairytales place most emphasis on the middle part of the story, which the storyteller can dramatize to maintain the audience's attention. The wrap-up occurs very near the end of the story session: "So the prince married the goose girl, and they all lived happily ever after." When you are talking to an audience, you need to maintain their interest right from the start and keep the tension high. Good storytellers know this and pace their narratives accordingly.

A similar three-stage technique is used to create dramatic tension in most books, plays and films. Let's study a variety of narrative forms to see how the 'story mountain' model can apply to them. Note how plays fit this dramatic analysis very neatly. The novel form is longer and can introduce subsidiary events (fractal patterns) which echo and reinforce the main plot.

Oedipus Rex (Play by Sophocles, 429 BC)
Initial scene: Oedipus lives with his (foster) parents.
New event: The oracle foretells that he will kill his father.
Hero's response: Oedipus decides never to return home.
Dramatic event: He meets his real father unknowingly and slays him in a fight.
Hero's action: Oedipus succeeds as king of Thebes and marries the queen.
Crucial climax: Tiresias reveals Oedipus' true parentage as

prince of Thebes.

Heroic re-action: Oedipus blinds himself in remorse and shame.

Resolution: Oedipus and his daughter wander in exile.

Outcome / Sequel: His family are tragically doomed.

The Crucible (Play by Arthur Miller, 1953)

Initial scene: A strict religious community riddled with hypocrisy.

New factor: Abigail denounces John's wife as a witch.

Hero's response: John, a prominent citizen, defends his wife.

Dramatic event: The girls become hysterical and make further accusations.

Hero's action: John rejects Abigail when she declares her love for him.

Crucial event: Abigail and her friends accuse John himself of sorcery.

Heroic re-action: John faces his death with noble demeanour.

Resolution: The girls are discredited in the community.

Outcome: Subsequent witch-hunts are suspect.

Pride and Prejudice (Novel by Jane Austen, 1813)

Initial scene: Five unmarried sisters live at home.

New factor: A regiment of soldiers arrives in town.

Heroine's response: Elizabeth flirts with Wickham: her heart is touched.

(Sub-plot: Bingley falls in love with the eldest sister, Jane.)

Dramatic event: Darcy is smitten with Elizabeth and proposes.

Heroine's action: Elizabeth rejects him with brutal but misplaced honesty.

(Sub-plot: Bingley and Jane are separated by misunderstandings.)

Crucial climax: The youngest sister Lydia falls for Wickham and they elope.

Heroine's re-action: Elizabeth is honest with Darcy; she realizes his true worth.

Resolution: Darcy sorts out Lydia's situation, saving the family reputation.

Outcome: Elizabeth and Darcy are happily united.

(Sub-plot: Bingley and Jane also marry.)

Harry Potter Series (Books and films by JK Rowling, 1997–2007)

Initial scene: Harry lives in his uncle's understairs cupboard.

New factor: A messenger discloses that his parents were wizards.

Hero's response: Harry goes to learn magic at Hogwarts School.

Dramatic event: The evil Voldemort discovers his whereabouts.

Hero's action: Harry trains hard to develop his skills at sorcery.

Crucial climax: Voldemort launches a mortal attack on Harry.

Hero's re-action: Harry chooses death to destroy his enemy.

Resolution: Voldemort is finally vanquished.

Outcome: Almost everyone good is saved, including Harry.

The story structure is similar in every case, although the content will differ according to the type of narrative. If you are writing a novel, the central events will probably occur about two-thirds of the way through the book. This gives you time to build suspense, and still have space to develop the story and wrap up loose ends. Your readers should care about the main characters, and want to know what happened to them afterwards. For scriptwriters, the action may start earlier but the denouement typically comes a little later, about three-quarters of the way through. This is because plays and films rely on visual information. The audience only know what they have witnessed: you can't include intro-spection, so you have to show things happening instead. The dependence on dialogue limits what background information can be provided. It is correspondingly harder to maintain interest after the plot twist has been revealed.

Note: A similar narrative pattern identified by Joseph Campbell is the 'hero's journey'. The story starts when something forces the protagonist to leave home. They meet a wise mentor who helps them prepare for their journey. Next, the hero/ine encounters a challenge which reflects the main drama to come. They surmount this obstacle and become stronger in the process. Eventually, they battle a monster – or plumb the depths of the underworld – and gain a prize. This reward may take the form of outward wealth (treasure) or inner riches (enlightenment). Finally, they return home: everything is familiar but they are subtly changed. This affects their future experience, and can provide a link to further stories. Many classical myths follow the template of the hero's journey. Modern novelists and scriptwriters often use this model as inspiration for their work.

Building Suspense

Once upon a time, there was a dragon that terrorized the land.
 One day, a brave knight came along and heard about it.
 He killed the dragon and married the princess.

Did you like that story? Or was it a bit short? Actually, it hardly merited the title of 'story'. The basic facts above could have been a Reuters report. Good journalism involves expanding the bare bones and putting them into context. A newspaper article might include quotes from an eye-witness report and a bit of background information. ('"It demands a maiden each day for dinner," said the Mayor. Teenage girls are the favourite food for this type of dragon.') Great journalism almost always involves a little human interest. ('"Most of my friends have been eaten already. It's very upsetting because I might be next," said Angelina, the Mayor's daughter.')

To make this into a good story, you need to elaborate the plot. As a storyteller, you can use a little poetic license: embroider the basic facts with dramatic detail. Perhaps we could have made it slightly more interesting. A good way of doing that would be to introduce some suspense. How about this:

Once upon a time, there was a dragon which terrorized the land. Its fiery breath melted the thickest armour; its scaly skin would blunt the sharpest blade. The dragon's favourite food was human flesh. Many strong men had gone to slay the serpent, but none ever returned. Their shields had only served as barbecue trays...

By expanding the text, we have turned it into a story. As the old storytelling edict goes:

Make 'em laugh; make 'em cry; make 'em wait...

Which leads us on to...

Rule of Threes

One of the best ways of building suspense is the 'rule of threes'. This is so ingrained into our storytelling culture that audiences almost expect it. Setbacks are an integral part of the quest. If the hero succeeds at once, people are slightly disappointed. If a mission is worth undertaking, then surely it has to be harder than opening the biscuit tin.

There is a story about Robert the Bruce, an early king of Scotland. His army was decimated and he was forced to flee in disguise. At length he came to a peasant's cottage and begged for shelter. The poor woman had no idea who he was, but she kindly agreed to let him sit by her fire. There was just one condition: would he watch her oatcakes bake on the griddle whilst she was milking?

This was quite a comedown for a king, but Robert was thankful for any refuge. He wrapped himself in his damp cloak and sat huddled by the hearth. He stayed so still that a spider came out and attached its web to the toe of his shoe. It had nearly finished when he moved slightly and the web was torn apart. Undaunted, the spider scuttled to another point and started to work again. Once more its strand came loose, and once more it had to begin again. This time it chose a better anchor, and managed to weave a beautiful web. The king was entranced: he completely forgot about the oatcakes. When she came in, the peasant woman cuffed his ears for letting them burn. Robert was so inspired by the spider's perseverance that he rallied his troops and won back his throne.

The 'rule of threes' is one of the strongest tools in the wordsmith's box. Think about all the best stories you know. How often does the hero succeed on the first attempt? If things were too easy, it would not be an interesting story – nor a very inspiring one. After all, we want to be able to identify with the challenge, and we often don't get things right first time around. Instead, the protagonist has to 'try and try and try again'. It is usually not until the last attempt that they manage to achieve their goal. Third time lucky, as the saying goes. Sometimes this is shown by three siblings attempting the same task. A Celtic myth relates how Finn McCool and his brothers are resting in the forest. The eldest goes to find water, but is accosted at the well by a hideous hag. He rejects her rudely, and returns to the others empty-handed. The second brother suffers a similar experience and also fails to get a drink. Young Finn takes his turn, and greets the grandam with a hearty kiss. She transforms into a beautiful woman, the spirit of Ireland, and nominates him as the future king. In this story, the three brothers represent different ways of dealing with the same situation. Finn is the only one who shows a generous heart, which qualifies him to rule the land.

Another way of using the 'rule of threes' is to show the main protagonist in a series of similar adventures. Each incident foreshadows the proceedings of their final adventure. As a child, the hero rescues his sister from a village pond: years later, he battles a sea-monster to rescue the princess. The early adventures demonstrate the qualities and behaviour that he will need in his final task. 'Fractal' patterns foreshadow the climatic event. These minor incidents reflect the unfolding of the story, just as each frond of a fern is a microcosm of the larger leaf. Compare this structure to the 'story mountain' that we talked about earlier.

When you are making stories, think of how you could use the 'rule of threes'. What challenge or opportunity does your protagonist face? How might they fail at first, without getting destroyed? What will be different on the attempt when they finally succeed? How does this relate to the message of your story? Remember to keep it relevant and realistic, to maintain the audience's interest. This threefold approach also lets you experiment with different solutions to the problem. You might even find that you change your story as a result of what you learn.

Five Finger Technique

Speakers and storytellers need to memorize their material in a way that facilitates recall. There are several things which you need to include when telling a story. An easy way to remember them is the 'five finger technique'. This is a simple mnemonic system I have developed which uses your own hand to help recall everything you need to know. You can apply it in many different situations where you have to remember things. Because it is so simple, it is especially useful in situations where you have to make a speech or tell a story.

The trick is to associate each finger with something that you will find easy to remember. Start by making a 'thumbs up' gesture. Your fingers are in a fist and your thumb sticks upright. What does this gesture mean to you? In Western culture it symbolizes something along the lines of, "I'm all right, Jack." This will be the starting point of your story, when everything is in balance: the status quo. You can make similar associations for each of your other digits. Your index finger is used for pointing the way. Your middle finger is the major (biggest) one. Your ring finger symbolizes relationships. Your little finger extends your reach. Your hand is a portable tool which provides five prompts to shape your story. Secretly count off your points before you begin, to make sure that you tell an effective tale.

To memorize a story or plan a speech, use your fingers to build a set of simple associations. Your thumb represents the status quo. This is how things are when the story starts. Your forefinger indicates going somewhere new. This is the 'inciting incident' which changes everything. Your middle finger comprises the major part of the story. This should have three cumulative incidents which build to the climax ('rule of threes'). Your ring finger recalls the resolution of story, including any emotional consequences. Your little finger shows the outcome, including any links to the future. If you have a good punchline, put it here.

To see how the five finger technique works in action, let's apply it to another familiar story: *Little Red Riding Hood*.

Thumb: Red Riding Hood visits her grandmother every Sunday.
Forefinger: A wolf learns where she is going and hides in grand-mother's bed.
Middle finger:
1) Grandmother, what big eyes you have!
   (All the better to see you with, my dear.)

2) Grandmother, what big ears you have!
   (All the better to hear you with, my dear.)
3) Grandmother, what big teeth you have!
   The wolf jumps up to EAT her...

Ring finger: Luckily Grandmother keeps a woodchopper beside her stove.

Little finger: The big bad wolf never bothers her again.

Do you see how easy it is to remember?

Now let's apply it to a folktale where you might need to memorize a bit more detail: *Jack and the Beanstalk*.

Thumb: Status quo. Jack lived with his mother in a tiny cottage. They were so poor that they only had one cow.

Forefinger: Pointing the way. One day Jack's mother told him to take the cow to market. On the way he met an old man and exchanged the cow for five 'magic' beans.

Middle finger: Main part of story. In the night a great beanstalk sprouted. Jack climbed up and above the clouds he found a giant's castle. He stole a bag of gold coins.

For a while Jack and his mother could buy food. When the money ran out, Jack climbed the beanstalk again. He stole the giant's goose which laid golden eggs.

Now Jack and his mother were rich. But one day Jack decided to climb the beanstalk for a third time.. He stole a magic harp and the giant chased him.

Ring finger: Resolution. Jack tumbled down the beanstalk and called for his mother to bring the axe. He cut the beanstalk and the giant fell to the ground. Phew!

Little finger: Outcome. Jack and his mother lived in a little cottage. They only had one goose: but that goose laid eggs made of pure gold...

Let's see how we can develop a longer version of a well-known fairytale: *Beauty and the Beast*.

Status quo: In a deep, dark forest... in a great grey castle... in a lonely tower... there lived a hideous beast.

Precipitating incident: One stormy night, a merchant came knocking at the castle door. He had lost his way and was seeking shelter. The Beast, ashamed of his appearance, kept out of sight; but he arranged for the man to be fed and given a comfortable bed. Next morning, as he was leaving, the merchant plucked a rose from the garden. Furious at this presumption, the Beast leapt out and seized him. The terrified man explained that the flower was a gift for his daughter, and the Beast agreed to spare him on condition that this girl come to take his place.

Main Story: When Beauty arrived at the castle, the Beast supplied her with everything she might want: fine food, rich clothes, and of course the rose garden to walk in. Each night he joined her at supper, although he would not eat for fear that his great jaws might disgust her. Gradually she became accustomed to his presence, and even began to enjoy his company. They talked together of many things: music, art and books. The Beast gave her a piano and offered her use of his splendid library.

But although she had everything she needed, and much to occupy her mind, Beauty still missed her family. The Beast grew to care for the girl, and he was saddened by her obvious distress. At last he offered to let her go home, on condition that she return within three days: "For I would die without you."

Resolution: The girl returned home, and was delighted to see her family. A week flew past, and her father pressed her to stay. But when she was free to choose, Beauty found that she longed for her new life. She returned to the castle, but the Beast was nowhere to be seen. She ran from room to room, calling his name. At last she went out into the rose garden. There she found him, lying on a path by the stream where they had often walked. Now that she had lost him, Beauty realized how much the Beast meant to her. She knelt down and kissed his cold damp fur. Then she buried her face in her hands and wept.

After a moment she felt a hand on her shoulder…

Outcome: In a green forest, in a great castle, in a tall tower, a handsome prince embraced his radiant bride.

This version of the folk-tale follows the five finger technique of story structure to elaborate on the basic plot. By taking the Beast's viewpoint, it elicits sympathy for the monstrous protagonist. The central section also obeys the 'rule of threes': the Beast attempts to supply in turn the needs of body, mind and spirit. It is only when he finally grants her freedom that Beauty realizes she has grown to love him. Once she recognizes him as her soulmate, his outer appearance transforms to reflect his inner worth.

Now it's over to you. Think of a story you could tell: perhaps a funny thing that happened last weekend. Use the five finger technique to structure your story.

1 Starting situation
2 Inciting incident
3 So… but… then…
4 Resolution!
5 Wind-up.

Next, think of a story you want to pitch: say, the case for a new drinks machine at work. Use the five finger technique to construct your argument.

1 Initial position
2 What's changed
3 Tried this… but… and…
4 Present solution!
5 Catchphrase.

So you've been working hard and business is booming. You deserve a pay rise, but your manager doesn't seem to have noticed. How could you tell that story?

1 When I started this job...
2 Then the business began to change...
3 I responded by... but customers said... so I introduced...
4 And look at the sales figures!
5 So I would like X.

See how well the five finger story technique works? Instead of simply complaining or trying to bulldoze your solution, you've taken the audience on a journey where they actually come up with the same conclusion. It's an incredibly powerful way of persuading people to do what you want. And you've put your case in a pocket-sized format where you can take it and tell it anywhere: in the lobby, in the conference room, at your annual review. If your story is good, you'll soon hear people telling it for you.

Your turn!

Simile or Metaphor

So you've chosen your story and identified your main characters. You've planned the outline and plotted how to build suspense. Now you need to focus on bringing your work to life. How can you make your writing vivid? What can you do to ensure that your readers or listeners are really with you? How can you bring this imaginary world to life?

Stories are just a string of words. What makes them so powerful? Partly it's the way they appeal to all the senses. You hear a sequence of sounds, or see a line of squiggles on the page, and your mind makes them into an adventure. When you hear a story, you see things in your mind's eye. Listening is an active skill: you construct a complete fantasy world by creating pictures in your image-ination. Your other senses are evoked too: sound, smell, touch and taste. The way this works is through description, simile and metaphor.

Which of these sentences is most powerful?
My manager is being mean.
My supervisor acts like a witch.
My boss is an ogre.

The first example is a description. It uses an adjective to give us a clear message.

The second sentence is a simile. It says that something is 'like' (similar to) something else. A simile evokes a stronger emotional response.

The third example is a metaphor. It makes a literal claim: that one thing is actually something else. This statement creates a vivid picture in the listener's mind.

A simile or metaphor doesn't just have to be a noun. Let's try some more examples.
The horse galloped incredibly fast.
The falcon dropped like a stone.
The greyhound shot across the finishing line.

Allow each phrase in turn to manifest in your imagination. What do you feel reading the description? How effective is the simile? Does the metaphor bring an image into your mind? Think about the effect your words will have on your listeners, and use these tools carefully.

Voice and Viewpoint

Whose story is this anyway? Are you relating something that happened to you? Is this fiction, but you've decided to use the first person ('I') to make it more immediate? Or are you describing events that happened to someone else? If so, you may want to tell the story from their viewpoint. Can you see inside the mind of your main character? Or do you want to be able to show the action from several different perspectives? Decide which angle you think would be most effective for your story.

There is not a 'best' way to tell a story: different approaches suit different types of anecdote. Decide how you want the audience to feel as the story develops. How do you respond to the following sentences?

> "The man looked worried."
> "Sam felt scared."
> "I was terrified."

You probably found the last sentence most moving. This is because people are neurologically programmed to respond to intense emotion. The individual report – 'I' – evokes your personal involvement.

Now compare these statements:
> "I felt as though I'd been punched in the stomach."
> "His mouth dropped open with shock."

Note how the first sentence elicits an almost physical sensation, even though the second actually gives you more factual information.

If you want your audience to respond strongly to your story, you might choose a personal viewpoint: 'I saw it happen'. Relating 'my story as it happened to me' makes your account much more emotional. This direct narrative makes it easier for the audience to identify with the feelings you recount. However, using 'I' limits you to relating the main character's experience: you cannot tell the audience things which 'I', the narrator, do not know – or choose to tell you! For writers, it can also be hard to maintain the 'voice' of your central character, especially if they have a colloquial accent or idiosyncratic speech.

"I didn't know what the heck 'e was up to, but sure as horses, it meant trouble."

Y'all see what I mean, now?

The third person perspective – "Goldilocks lived in a house at the edge of the woods" – lets you round out your story with more background detail. As the narrator, you are omniscient: you can tell your audience anything you want them to know. However, it is most effective to stay within the viewpoint of your central character. Your listeners should never know more than your hero/ine. This means you can build dramatic tension, especially in a story where you want the denouement to be a surprise. Of course, it can be hard to expand your plot using only a single viewpoint. Use dialogue or reported speech to let other characters explain their opinions and actions. Novelists sometimes have a series of narrators, alternating the viewpoint between chapters. This lets them give information from a variety of perspectives.

Another approach is the 'narrator voice'. This is when you speak in the first person, telling us about things that happened to someone else: "I saw him from my window, trudging through the rain..." It is the method used in *The Great Gatsby* where we learn about the main character from his neighbour. This enables you to elicit sympathy for your subject, but also to include information that they could not possibly have known. This technique can be particularly effective for speakers and storytellers. Raconteurs often use the narrator voice, claiming that anecdotes happened to 'a friend of mine'. Speakers can also use the second person very effectively, as you see here: this helps your audience to identify with what you are saying.

Whichever perspective you choose, the most important person in your story is the 'protagonist'. This is the character whom your audience should care about most. You introduce subsidiary figures as necessary to develop your story. Sometimes you may create a character to contrast with the main personality. Your protagonist needs an antagonist to provide dramatic conflict. This opposition is most effective if the two characters also share some features. The darker figure then becomes the alter ego of the lighter one. Each needs the other: together they function as a complementary pair. Batman needs the Joker before he can save Gotham City. Jane Eyre's repressed sensuality is expressed by Rochester's mad wife.

Even though we want them to win, your hero doesn't have to be faultless: in fact, the opposite is true. Perfect people are deeply irritating. Your characters don't have to behave nicely all the time. It is because they are scared that we admire their bravery; when they tell petty lies that they are most humane. In art as in life, we tend to like people whom we can empathize with. Often we identify with someone, not in spite of their bad points, but because of them. The evil knight might be a lot more fun than the virtuous prince. After all, these faults represent less desirable aspects of our selves. By allowing your characters to have flaws, you are making your story more relevant to your audience.

Developing Dialogue

Let your characters speak for themselves. It's a great way of bringing them to life. Whether you're a speaker, writer or storyteller, dialogue is a great tool to have in your box.

When you are doing dialogue, try to create a different 'voice' for each of your characters. Developing speech patterns is an effective method of evoking personality. Think about what vocabulary they might use. Perhaps you can differentiate them with a verbal tag line ("... is it, like?"). This works for both writing and storytelling: it helps to have a 'catchphrase' to distinguish your characters. This is often easier than putting on exaggerated regional accents.

Composing dialogue is harder than you might think. The problem is that good dialogue is not actually realistic. Try eavesdropping on someone's conversation: you'll find it is full of repetition and odd references. Characters in a story have to speak much more purposefully than real people! Whatever you feel about dialogue, good writers have to do a lot of it. Modern novels consist of about 1/3 action; 1/3 description or introspection; and 1/3 dialogue. The same proportions apply pretty well within an individual passage. See how well the different parts balance each other:

> 'It was cold for July, and the pavement was still wet with last night's rain.
> Susan was trimming the geraniums in her front garden when she heard footsteps.
> "Good day, Mr Weatherby," she called brightly. "You're up early this morning!"'

Speakers and storytellers will vary these ratios depending on their skill with voices, but convincing speech is an important part of their repertoire.

Dialogue in a speech or story should follow five basic principles:

1. Dialogue should start from where you are. It is cheating to include background information in the guise of conversation. "As I was getting the bus home from my cleaning job in Whitechapel, which I took to make ends meet after my husband left me for his mistress, I saw..." Nooooo!

2. Use speech to go somewhere. In other words, it must further the action or provide important information about events or characters. The best dialogue uses short snappy sentences, without 'umms' and 'ahhs. Your readers don't want to spend time on irrelevant drivel.

3. Most important: Show, not tell! Use setting to indicate emotion and to dramatize the scene. You can even use it to indicate who is speaking.
   "It's only for a year," Jack said.
   Emma turned towards the window.
   "I wish you luck, for sure."
'Show, not tell' is the cardinal rule of good writing!

4. Relationships depend on actions, not words. Characters reveal their real motives and feelings by what they do. This may confirm or contradict what they say...

5. Varying voices: Short typical phrases are a lot easier to keep up than complex accents.

(Did you spot how I used the 'five finger technique' to help you remember these points?)

A good way to develop dialogue is to assign a prop to each character. Choose something that they would use or wear: a hat, a scarf, a jacket or pair of shoes. Use this item to help you 'get into character' and develop a voice for each persona. The Trickster exercise, 'Talk It Through', elaborates this technique.

Archetypal Figures

How well do you know your characters? It's important to understand the people in your story. Writers in particular can spend a long time developing their protagonists. This is where you use those 'getting to know' questionnaires (see the worksheet in Part III of this book). What is this character's name? What is their role in this story? What motivates him or her? What do they look like? Their strengths and weaknesses? Their likes and dislikes? Their favourite colour? Their favourite food?...

Knowing this sort of detail can make your characters more realistic. Your audience want characters whom they can recognize. This makes them more sympathetic to the story. After all, that's the only reason they pay attention: they care about what happens to these people. They want to know what happens next. What's more, your listeners like characters who they can identify with. Familiar figures are more likely to reflect their own experience of life. If you're telling an anecdote, make the central character similar to the people in your audience. You may have to twist the original tale, but this will make it much more effective. When you're trying to motivate a group of female call centre operatives, don't tell the story of *Little Lord Fauntleroy*. Not even if it was your favourite book as a child. To be an effective speaker, you must always keep your listeners and their interests in mind.

Your characters are hopefully original, but they must also be believable. They must have convincing personalities. They probably need to look the part too. The audience must see them as people they might actually meet. You achieve this by combining unique features with common characteristics which are instantly recognizable. This is because we all tend to categorize people in similar ways. We use 'stereotypes' to help us deal with the people we encounter. These stereotypes are not fully evolved images, but merely an automatic way of storing initial information. Psychologists believe that we base our perceptions of others on such stereotypical character outlines.

The same characters recur in stories from around the world. You recognize these figures when you encounter them: the hero, the princess, the wise man and so on. Myths and legends, books and films all feature common character types. Although details of their appearances vary, you know how they are likely to behave. When you are telling a story, these stereotypes provide a convenient narrative shorthand. You invoke a set of attributes, and avoid the need for detailed description. Realistic characters are based on these universal figures called 'archetypes'. So the first question on your character sheet should really be, 'What's their archetype?'

Archetypes are universal figures which arise spontaneously in our minds. They are outline forms which are innate in the human psyche. Each figure consists of a constellation of common attributes. Their individual features are filled with material from your personal experience. Your image of a 'good mother' draws on your own encounters with mothering. When you tell a story which features a good mother, you will describe her in line with your experience. The old woman next door doesn't smile, so she is mean and malevolent. You fear the witch because of folk-tales you once heard. Your story may have a clever girl, a trickster and a tramp: they will be your creations, yet they will also draw on your reader's expectations of these roles.

Archetypal figures are familiar and reassuringly predictable. You use them to categorize people that you meet, both in stories and in real life. There are twelve main archetypal figures, as shown in the table. They have many different faces, but all are variations of these twelve fundamental characters. You recognize them when you meet them: the princess and the wicked witch, the hero and the trickster. Their names reflect their basic characteristics, but they can manifest in many ways. The mother can be a teacher, nurse or Good Samaritan. The trickster can be a dangerous enemy but a useful ally.

As a wordsmith, you can draw on archetypal figures and the expectation that they arouse. When you introduce a character, drop hints about their role in the narrative. Is this a wise mentor, or a villain whose advice will jeopardize the hero/ine's quest? How does your central character respond to this meeting? When you evoke an archetype, you don't have to explain all of your character's thoughts and actions. You can assume that the reader knows more than has actually been said: the character is just behaving according to type. Conversely, you can play with the reader's expectations and assumptions. Silver hair may not be a metaphor for acquired knowledge; high heels may ornament a razor-sharp mind.

The archetypes can be broadly divided into male and female figures, although they are all potentially present within each of us. A woman can play the trickster to get what she wants; a man may mother his best friend through difficult times. Masculine and feminine energies (animus and anima) are counterparts and coexist within everyone. Broadly speaking, the female figures are concerned with the personal or domestic domain; the male characters are associated with action in the public arena.

Another division is between light and dark figures. These are not simply powers of good and evil: they are contrasting but complementary forces. The light figures are generally seen as 'good': the princess, the hero, the wise man. The dark figures are more ambivalent, although they too can create as well as destroy. A man may have to act like an ogre to get things done. In patriarchal societies, a clever girl does not reveal the full extent of her powers. Fairytales say that if you do not honour the ogre or witch, they will consume you. In other words, you must integrate all these aspects within yourself to become a fully developed human being. The true hero must recognize the monster within himself.

The table below shows the twelve main archetypal figures. They fall into three main categories: young, mature and old. Within each category, there are both light and dark figures. Each of the archetypes has many possible manifestations: some modern characters are listed in Part III, 'Contemporary Figures'. You can learn more about archetypal figures in my book *LifeWorks*.

The stories in this book have been arranged according to their main character. But archetypes need their counterparts in order to manifest. The hero is aimless without a princess to rescue; the good mother needs a hungry urchin to feed. In each tale you will recognize variations of other basic archetypal figures. This will give you more ideas for your own storytelling.

The Twelve Archetypes

	Female	Male
Young		
Light	Princess	Noble Youth
Dark	Clever Girl	Urchin
Mature		
Light	Good Mother	Hero/ine
Dark	Wild Woman	Trickster
Old		
Light	Grandam	Wise One
Dark	Witch	Ogre

Doing The Work

In the next part of this book, you will find a wide selection of tales for telling. The stories are presented in groups, based on their main characters. At the end of each section, you will find a short task. These will help you to develop your own narrative techniques. You can do them with a partner as a storyworking challenge, or on your own as a creative exercise. In either case you will probably want a pencil and paper to record your responses. If you decide to talk, let each person speak for three or four minutes; then spend a minute giving feedback. If you want to write, read through the exercise and then set a timer for ten minutes. With writing, the key rule is simply to get going. Once you begin, keep your hand moving constantly over the page. Don't stop to edit or evaluate what you've written until the end of the exercise. This ability to produce script is the secret tool of the true writer. Don't wait for inspiration to strike, nor pause for the perfect word. You can't cut your cloth until it's woven: there will be plenty of time later on for amendments.

Part II: Tales For Telling

In this part of the book you'll find many stories. Some of them will strike you as especially meaningful: these are the tales which resonate with your personal story. Others might move you in a different way: these may reflect a life choice that you could consider. Some have a clear moral or message; others might prompt you to reflect on their meaning. Some of them stick to the storytelling guidelines described above; others play fast and loose with the rules. Each of them is a story that you might choose to use. All of them are tales from which you can learn.

The stories here come from many different sources. Some draw on myths and legends from around the world; others evoke more contemporary times and places. They have been grouped together by their main protagonist: the archetypal figure whom the central character represents. If you are a public speaker, these stories will provide a wide variety of source material. Leaders and managers will find a rich source of anecdotes for presentations. Trainers and coaches can use these tales to illustrate teaching points. Therapists can use them to deepen understanding of archetypal roles – the 'games people play'. For writers, they will help you to develop your own characters more fully. 'Business Applications' in Part III shows you how to use these stories in a professional context.

Whatever your needs and purpose, you will find stories here to inspire, to teach and to amuse. Enjoy!

The Princess

A princess is a very special person.

Elf Maid

At breakfast this morning, my little brother said:
"You look like an elf princess."
"Really?" I smiled, biting my lip and widening my eyes.
"Yes. Your ears are sticking out of your hair."
Thanks a lot, bro.

Five lines: expectations raised and demolished → story!

A Real Princess

There once lived a girl who was a real princess, but she had the misfortune to be born into a peasant family. Her parents were coarse and common and poor: they would not buy the fine frocks and fancy shoes which befit a princess. Her house was small and mean and badly furnished. Her face was covered with freckles and her hair was carroty curls. In fact, everything about her life was excruciatingly embarrassing. The only thing the princess cared for was her little brother, who adored her.

One day the girl was walking into town when she met a gipsy woman selling ribbons and laces.

"Come and look! Try and buy!" the pedlar called.

The girl stopped and fingered the pretty things, but she had no money to buy even a bow.

"Oh! If only I could!" she sighed. "But I simply can't afford them!"

"Another day, my dear." The gypsy smiled and closed her basket. A little way down the rough path, she stumbled and fell.

42

Now, the girl had a good heart and could be charming to anyone who was not immediate family, so she ran to help the old woman up.

"Thank you, my dear," said the pedlar. "Let me give you a gift for your trouble. This is a magic thread and it will grant what you desire." And she pulled a yellow ribbon from her pack and gave it to the girl.

The girl didn't really believe in magic but she thought it would be polite to play along, so she exclaimed,

"What fun! Well, I wish to be as beautiful as the dawn!"

She looked down and saw that her shabby skirt had changed into a designer dress. On her feet were silver sandals with diamante buckles. Her hair hung smooth and blonde about her shoulders, and her arms were fair and freckle-free.

"That's your first wish," said the gypsy. "Choose the others carefully, for you have just three."

By the time she had finished admiring herself, the old woman had disappeared.

The princess carried on walking into the town. When she came to the main square she saw a group of her friends sitting on the wall.

"Hey! Look at me!" she called to them. But the other girls did not recognize her, and would not answer. She felt hurt and became angry, calling them nasty names. Before long, she was standing on her own in the street. Even when she was stuck with her dreadful family she had never felt more lonely.

"They're just jealous," she told herself. "I need to be rich as well as beautiful. Then I can mix with the proper sort of people. I wish that my house was full of gold!"

She pulled off her high-heeled sandals and ran home as fast as she could. When she got to her house, she saw that it was overflowing with golden coins. They glinted through the windows and spilled out of the doorway. And there, sticking out from the pile of coins was one small foot. Her baby brother had been crushed under the pile of money. She ran and tugged at his little leg but he did not move. His tiny toes were as cold as the metal around him.

The girl sank to the ground and started to sob. Through her tears, without thinking at all, she cried, "Oh! How I wish there was someone in the world who loved me!"

There was a trickling sound, and when she looked up, the gold coins were melting away like snow in springtime. The magic knew best how to do its work. Soon her little brother was lying there asleep in the sunshine. The boy opened his eyes and stretched out his arms towards her. She snatched him up into her lap and her long ginger hair hung like a curtain around him. At that moment she was surely the happiest person in the whole world.

'Be glad of what you've got': learning to be thankful is a favourite subject for stories. Current writings on mindfulness and gratitude are simply reworking a traditional theme.

Sulky Sedna

There once lived a girl called Sedna. She was very lovely to look at. Her black hair made a braid as thick as a man's wrist. Her eyes slanted slightly and her skin seemed always touched by the golden sun. News of her beauty spread, and many men came to court her. But Sedna was proud of her looks. She thought she was too good for any of them.

When a new suitor arrived, she would laugh in his face.

"What makes you think I'd look at a boy like you?"

Her braid would dance between her hips as she walked away.

One day, however, a stranger came to town. He was tall and dark and beak-nosed. Sedna came home one day and found him sitting on the wall outside her house.

The stranger smiled at the girl, and at once there was a

complicity between them. They began talking and she found his manner easy, if not a little arrogant. She invited him inside and offered him drinks. When her father came home, the stranger said that he had heard of Sedna's beauty and had come to see it was true. He explained that he was rich and influential in his own land. If Sedna would marry him, she would want for nothing. She would sleep on a bed of the finest feathers, have all the delicacies she wanted to eat, and have company wherever she went.

"Sedna is the loveliest girl I have ever seen," he ended. "She will finally be treated as she deserves."

Sedna was flattered and intrigued. She had always felt too good for her native town. This was her chance to have the life she deserved. Although her father counselled caution, she was not prepared to wait. She wished to leave with the handsome stranger as soon as possible.

"Please let me go, Daddy," she pleaded. "You know what a wonderful opportunity this is for me. Please, please, please."

Sedna's father could not deny this opportunity for his beloved daughter. Finally, he agreed and the pair were married the very next day. They set off in fine style, and their smiles and promises did not soothe the old man's lonely heart.

Some weeks passed, and there was no word from Sedna. Her father became increasingly concerned. One day, he set out to look for her. He travelled for some distance, and at last came to the place where the stranger lived. The road wound up a rocky hill, and came to an end above a cliff overlooking the sea. There was no fine house to be seen, only a tumbledown heap of stones. The father crept up and peered inside. To his horror, there lay his lovely daughter curled upon an old mattress. She was surrounded by dirty dishes, and mice scuttled around the floor.

Sedna heard his gasp and opened her eyes. She lifted her hands piteously towards him and began to sob. She had been so deceived: her husband was rich in lands but not in money. It was true that she wanted for nothing, but this was not what she had thought married life would be like. Her husband was not a real man: he certainly didn't deserve a girl like her.

Sedna's father was distraught. He had given consent for his daughter to marry a demon. Swiftly they made plans together for her escape. Sedna gathered together some jewelry and a few clothes. Her father picked up her bag and carried it outside. Sedna huddled low beside him, and they set off down the narrow clifftop road.

Suddenly Sedna's husband appeared, standing in the middle of the path before them. He stretched out his arms to both sides, completely blocking the way. He seemed much bigger, here on his own territory, and now he was furious.

"Where do you think you're going?" he cried. "Sedna swore to stay with me, for better or for worse. I have kept my oath: I have loved and cherished her. I have given her everything that I promised, and more besides. And how has she repaid me? With taunts and sulks and slights. Now you would help her go back on her word. What right have you to take my wife away from me?"

The father saw the truth in this complaint and he was overcome with remorse.

Turning to his daughter, he said:

"Your husband is right. I should not come between you. Go and talk to him."

"No!" she shrieked. "Get on! Do as I say!"

Her voice cut his brain like a knife.

"Go!" he shouted. He pushed her hard, so she stumbled and fell on the stony ground. She clutched at her father's ankles, sobbing piteously. He kicked her away, trampling on her fingers so she screamed with pain.

His heart pounding, full of fear and shame, the old man sped away. Behind him, he glimpsed the husband leaning down towards his girl. He did not wait to see what would happen next.

This story has many messages. Beauty must love her Beast before he turns into a handsome prince. No father can protect his daughter forever. However special you are, you must cut your coat to fit your cloth.

The Inuit of North America say that Sedna married a sea-bird who took the form of a man. She has her own realm now, at the bottom of the ocean. Because of her hurt fingers, Sedna cannot comb her long hair. When the shamans visit they comb her tangled locks, and in return she sends seals to feed the people.

Poor Turkey Girl

In early times there lived a girl who was so poor that she earned her bread as a turkey-herd. Every morning she left her tumble-down home to collect the flocks of families richer than her own. She would drive them out into the plains and watch all day as they foraged among the dry grass. Sometimes she was so lonely that she talked to the birds.

"How I wish that I had a pretty dress," she would say. "And nice food, and a ribbon for my hair."

But although she was shabby, she had a kind heart and always looked after the birds in her care. Because of this, the turkeys were obedient and always came when she called.

One day the girl was driving her birds out of town when they passed a procession of youths and maidens. They were preparing for the spring festival of the Great Dance. No-one even noticed the drab little bird-herd. The girl watched them wistfully and chattered to the turkeys.

"How I wish I could attend," she cried. "But it is impossible that anyone so ugly should take part." Little did she suspect that her birds understood every word. They clustered together, gobbling and squawking. At last one of the biggest cocks strutted up to her. Fanning out his tail and the skirts of his wings, he spoke to her.

"Maiden mother," he announced, "We are thankful for your good care and have decided that you are worthy as anyone to attend the dance. Do as we say tonight and you shall join the festivities. But take care that you return to us in good time, lest we think that you have left us. Do not become harsh to us as others are to you now."

The girl was very surprised, but she found it quite natural to converse with her turkeys. When the sun set, they turned for home of their own accord. The big turkey escorted her into their hut and laid her wrap on the ground. In a moment it was transformed into a shimmering cape covered with gleaming feathers. The turkeys circled around her, clucking and grooming until her hair was brushed smooth and her skin burnished brightly. Then they began coughing up things they had found and swallowed: a necklace, ear pendants and many rings for her fingers.

When the girl was properly adorned, she thanked the birds delightedly. As she turned to leave they called after her:

"Maiden mother, know that we love you! Never forget us if your luck changes tonight! Remember our words and do not tarry too long!"

"I will remember," she cried, and rushed away into the night.

When she entered the main square, all eyes turned towards this beautiful stranger. Murmurs of appreciation ran through the crowd. The youths and maidens held out their hands and invited her to join their circle. Her heart was light and her smile dazzling as she danced.

The hours sped by and suddenly she saw that the sky was getting light. Breaking free, she slipped down an alley and hurried back towards the turkey hut. But meanwhile, the turkeys had begun to wonder why their maiden mother was gone so long.

"She has forgotten us," they said. "It is just as we feared. Now that she has good fortune, there will be no-one to look after us. We had better leave whilst we can."

The birds bustled out of the door which the girl had left open. They ran up the valley calling loudly to one another. By the time the girl arrived, they were long gone. Her cape was in tatters, her hair tangled, her skin dusty and dull. She was just Poor Turkey Girl once more.

This is a folktale told by the Zuni of New Mexico. It is reminiscent of Cinderella *– the best-known story in the world – but with a moral sting in the tail!*

Snowmaiden

Snowmaiden was the daughter of Fair Spring and red-nosed Old Frost. She was a quiet child, with fair skin and long blonde hair. She grew up in her father's icy kingdom, safe from the sun who might melt her with the heat of his passion.

On Snowmaiden's fifteenth birthday, the northern sky was filled with lights. After the festivities, her parents met to discuss the future. She could not live forever hidden from the world. Finally, they decided to entrust her to the care of an old peasant couple. One day, as the old people were walking in the woods, the man began to fashion a 'snow-maid'. To his astonishment, her eyes opened and she stepped towards him, a real live girl.

The old couple were delighted, and took Snowmaiden home to live with them. Yet day by day, as the spring sun warmed the land and the frost began to melt, she sought out cool shady places and remained pale.

One morning, some village girls and boys passed by the house and invited Snowmaiden to play with them. She hung back reluctantly from their games until the shepherd boy, Lel, began to play his flute. Then she allowed him to take her hand and joined the young people in their dance. From that time on, Lel the shepherd visited Snowmaiden every day. But though he grew to love her, he could feel no answering warmth from her heart. Finally, the day came when he asked another village girl to join him in the dance. Stricken with grief, Snowmaiden ran until she came to the edge of the forest. Throwing herself on the ground, she called to her mother for help: better to experience love for a brief moment than to live frozen for eternity.

Her mother took pity on her, and gave her a human heart. Placing a crown of snowdrops on her daughter's head, she warned her to guard herself from the sun's fiery gaze. But Snowmaiden was too happy to listen or care. Running back through the woods, she found Lel and threw her arms around him. Lel took her hands and whirled her in a joyous dance.

The sun rose higher in the cloudless spring sky, dispelling the early mists and melting the last patches of snow. Snowmaiden felt her feet starting to turn to water. Too weak to dance, she begged Lel to play her one last tune. As he did so, she sank to the ground and melted away. All that remained on the grass was her circlet of snowdrops.

Thus winter gives way to spring, and the warm sun kisses the earth and brings flowers. And Lel plays his flute and waits until the winter brings back his beloved Snowmaiden.

A Russian folk-tale which celebrates the passing of the seasons.

Exercise: Awaken The Senses

Your five senses are your birthright gift. Sight, sound, smell, taste and touch are the ways by which you connect with the world. One of the best ways to bring your work to life is by invoking these channels. As a wordsmith, you can constantly collect sensory impressions to use in your work. Wherever you go, try to be aware of the world around you. Walk like a cat: observe what is going on; sense the sounds and scents in the air. Savour the colours and noises and smells of everyday life. As your senses sharpen, your wordwork will improve.

We typically take in about 80% of our sensory information from the eyes. This leads to the old adage 'Seeing is believing'. The next most influential sense is hearing, accounting for nearly 20% of our data about the world. For most people, the other three senses – smell, taste and touch – are relegated to peripheral information. It is interesting that animals, who have a very different set of sensory priorities, are notably more astute in their evaluation of others!

This exercise will help you to focus your attention on these subsidiary senses. Take a small amount of strongly flavoured food – a tiny piece of dark chocolate is ideal; coffee or orange peel also work well. Sniff the food and inhale the aroma. Place the piece on your tongue, without chewing. Observe the texture in your mouth. See what flavours manifest on different parts of your tongue. As it warms up, see what different tastes and textures emerge. Observe how your mouth responds to this presence. Decide whether to chew or swallow. Afterwards, notice what flavours linger on the palate. Record your observations; see what thoughts and emotions they evoke. What images, similes or metaphors could you use to describe your experience?

(Read the famous passage in Marcel Proust's autobiography, *Swann's Way*, which describes how the smell of a madeleine cake transports him back to childhood memories.)

The Clever Girl

Clever girls can look after themselves.

Margarita's Dress

Margarita was a girl who knew her own mind. Which was just as well, since young men in her vicinity had a habit of losing theirs. Margarita had the face of an angel and the walk of a hussy. She had tilt eyes and plum lips and a curtain of jet-black hair. That girl was trouble on two legs and she ate boys' hearts for breakfast.

Until the morning that she met Pedro. The young man had just arrived in Lima and was acquainting himself with the place. As he sat drinking coffee in the market-place, he saw Margarita sauntering past. He looked her up and down, and his heart started jumping like a rabbit. Margarita gazed right back, and she was just as hooked. First there were smiles, then there were blushes, and before long the two of them were wild with love for each other.

News travels fast in a town. Before long, Margarita's father heard of the pair who met each morning in the market-place. Don Raimundo went along to see for himself, and he was not pleased with what he saw.

"That good-for-nothing!" he fumed. "He's got no skills, no talents, no way to make a living. The scoundrel just wants to marry into the family and live off me. Well, he can think again. Margarita is not getting a penny of dowry from me!"

And despite the pleadings and protestations of his wife, he remained adamantly against the match.

"She'll take nothing from my house," he declared. "If she insists on marrying the rascal, she will leave here in her petticoat."

Margarita took after her father enough to know that he would never change his mind. Luckily she had also inherited her mother's resourcefulness. So with that lady's help, she began at once to work on her wedding dress.

Together they sewed a chemise of sheer cotton. It was decorated with rows of Flanders lace that cost nearly 3,000 silver coins. The drawstring at her neck was a diamond chain worth ten times that amount, and the hem was weighted with pearls. When Margarita stepped out of her father's house on her wedding morning, her feet were bare but she was wearing her inheritance. Don Raimundo was eventually prevailed upon to give the couple his blessing. If he ever found out how he had been tricked, at least he didn't have to go back on his word.

A Peruvian history from the eighteenth century. When the old ladies of Lima think something is expensive, they say, "It costs more than Margarita's wedding dress!"

Love You Like Salt

The king was feeling tired. He had ruled his land for many years, and most would say he had been a good king. Under his hand, the poor had not gone hungry; the cattle had not wanted for water; the gods had not been neglected; the hearth-fires had not gone out. Yet now, the powers of leadership no longer gave him pleasure and he was starting to find his duties somewhat onerous.

He gathered his court around him. His wife was there too, and his comely daughters. The great throne faced the assembled throng. When the rustling of the crowd had died down, the king began to speak.

"Listen, and hear what I shall say. The time has come for me to go. Fear not, loyal subjects! – For I shall not go far. Four daughters have I, and each of them has a husband who has found favour with me. The daily rule of this land shall pass into

53

their capable hands. I shall retain only the crown title, and reside with each of them in turn to assist and advise them in their responsibilities. But first, it pleases me to set each of them a small test."

The king turned to his daughters who quickly threw themselves to their knees, displaying a pleasing sense of daughterly obedience and affection. He smiled at them benignly, and went on:

"To test your appreciation of your monarch, and hence your suitability to rule, tell me this: how do you perceive my royal self?"

The eldest daughter spoke first. Her voice trembled slightly, for there was much at stake here.

"Father, you are radiant as the crown you wear. You are precious to me as gold."

The king smiled, well pleased.

"Regally spoken, my dear. Into your rule I give the southern part of my kingdom, realm of rich grasslands under a golden sun."

The second daughter hobbled forwards slightly on her knees.

"Father, my life is guided by your wisdom. Your mind is like crystal, clear yet strong."

"Well spoken, my dear. To your rule I give the northern part of my kingdom, where the quartz quarries are to be found."

The third daughter spoke next, a little worried about her share.

"Father, your love is sweeter to me than any worldly treasure. I love you like sugar!"

"Sweetly spoken, my dear. To you I shall give the eastern seaboard, with its trading ports for cargoes of sugar and spice."

He turned expectantly to look at his youngest daughter. She was generally considered to be his favourite, although of course no man should show preference amongst his children. Luckily she was a calm creature who had never let such notions go to her head. Now she looked up at him with worried eyes.

"Father, I love you like salt."

The king frowned.

"Come, my darling, try again. Surely you can do better than that to please a father's heart!"

"Gold and crystal and sugar are very fine things, but I love you like salt."

Somewhere in the courtyard, someone sniggered. The old man rose to his feet in a fury.

"Is that all you have to say? I offer you a share of my kingdom, and you sneer at me? I would have made you queen over all after my death. As it is, your face no longer pleases me. Be gone from this house!"

The queen gasped, but said nothing. The other sisters looked at the ground. The youngest princess rose and gathered her cloak around her.

The crowd parted in silence as she left the room.

Over the following years, all came to pass as the king had planned. He handed over the day-to-day administration of the kingdom to his daughters. The king and queen retained the regal pomp associated with the crown. They visited their daughters in turn, spending a few weeks with each, although relations became a little strained. Sometimes the queen suspected they had outstayed their welcome, for the king could be somewhat didactic with his advice. At these times she would persuade him that he deserved a holiday from his administrative duties.

So it happened that one day the king and queen were travelling in a remote part of the land. They had only a small retinue, for as their daughters had pointed out, it was not necessary to spend much money on protecting such a beloved regent. Night was falling, and they had lost their way, for there were no familiar landmarks around them. They were glad to see lights in the distance, and these turned out to be the lamps of a large farm compound. A servant came out to greet them, and ushered the king and queen into a fine room with woven hangings and rush mats on the floor. They were seated at a long wooden table, lit by a hundred candles.

Presently the servant returned, bearing golden plates laden with steaming meat. Practically dribbling with hunger, the king picked up his fork and took a mouthful. Almost at once, his expression turned to one of disgust. Spitting out his food, he reached for his goblet and took a long draught. Spluttering, he slammed the glass back down and turned to his wife.

"We can't eat this food. It's disgusting, sickly sweet. There's something wrong with the water too."

At that moment a veiled woman entered the room. She was richly dressed, and obviously mistress of this house. Her voice was low and slightly mocking.

"Is the meal not to your liking?"

The king struggled to regain his composure, whilst the queen interjected swiftly.

"We are grateful for your hospitality. We have travelled far; we are hungry and thirsty. Sadly this food is too rich for our tongues."

"Yet it is served on golden plates, with crystal goblets, sweetened with much sugar." The woman lifted her veil and smiled at them. "Perhaps you would prefer some simple stew, seasoned with a little salt?"

How the queen cried to find her daughter safe and prosperous! How the king tugged his chin and paced around the room! How his daughter teased him when she caught him by the hand! For it was of course the youngest princess. She and her husband had made their own way in the world through wisdom and hard work. She had heard of the king's approach, and decided to teach him a lesson. Gold and crystal and sugar are all very well; but salt is the only seasoning which adds flavour to life.

Based on a tale from the Himalayan foothills. The conundrum in this story reminds me of King Lear. *Here the good daughter Cordelia is given a suitably happy ending.*

The Bear's Bride

In times before, there lived an Indian brave named Quissan. He loved a girl called Kinda who was beautiful as a flower in springtime. The two had been friends since childhood, and there was never a time when they did not walk together. But they could not marry, for they came of the same clan, and tribal law forbade their union.

Whilst they could be companions, life passed blissfully for the pair. But the time came when they were each of an age to marry. When they showed no interest in anyone else, their parents decided to separate them. Kinda was forbidden to leave the house, but she slipped out and met her lover in the woods. They decided to run away, preferring each other's company to anything else the world could offer.

The young couple walked deep into the mountain forests. In a secluded valley beside a stream they built a simple hut. Each day they foraged in search of food, being careful to avoid anyone from their village. At night they returned to the warmth of each other's arms. They were happy together, but as autumn approached, they felt the chill of the first frosts. Quissan resolved to return to the village for more supplies. Kinda chose to stay where she was, rather than face the wrath of her family.

Quissan's parents welcomed him home and asked about his long absence. When they heard how Kinda had become his wife, they were angry and afraid. They would not let him go back to the forest, for that would condone the forbidden union. The unhappy youth knew that Kinda would never return to the village alone. It was several weeks before he managed to slip away in search of his love.

When he came to the hut, he saw at once that it had been deserted for some time. He searched up and down the valley, calling out her name, but there was no sign of Kinda anywhere. After many days he gave up the search and returned to the village. This time he was greeted with much sympathy, but of course that did nothing to restore his lost love. Months passed, years gathered, and Kinda was seldom mentioned. But Quissan never forgot her, and believed in his heart that she would still be found.

One day he consulted a *skaga*, or medicine man, to see if he could throw any light on the situation. The *skaga* summoned a vision and saw Kinda sitting under a large cedar tree beside a lake. He told Quissan that she lived in this tree with a bear whom she had married and their two boys. Quissan lost no time in organizing a search party. The *skaga* led them to the lake he had seen, and there was Kinda sitting underneath the tree. They carried her home, and the people agreed that after such an ordeal, the two lovers might now be allowed to live together. But Kinda mourned her lost sons. She knew that the bear loved her and had sheltered her in the wilderness. It was dangerous for her to see him again, but she taught the hunters a song that the bear had composed to woo her. It went:

"I have taken a fair Haida maid as my wife.

"I will always be kind to her.

"I will give her berries from the hill,

"And roots from the ground to feed her.

"I will do all I can to please her.

"For her I made this song, and for her I sing it."

When they sang this, the bear was reminded of his love for Kinda. He came down from the cedar tree and talked to the hunters. He agreed to let the boys go to their mother, and they grew up amongst her people. One of them later returned to the bears, but the other married a village girl and had many children. To this day, their descendants live in the community. If they ever meet a bear, they sing the song that Kinda taught them, and the bear departs in friendship.

A Native American tale. This story was related to missionaries by a Haida man called Yak Quahu in 1873. (The couple's full names were Quiss-an-kweedass and Kind-a-wuss.) It helps us to understand the affinity between certain families and their totem animals.

The Waters of Life

Once there lived a Caliph and he had a wise old Vizier. The Vizier had two small children, a boy called Rumi who was brave as a warrior and a girl named Rasha who was bright as sunshine. When the old man knew that he was near to death, he feared for his children amidst the connivings of court life. So he arranged for them to go and live in a cottage in the middle of the woods. There they were raised by a loyal serving-woman who loved them as her own. The children grew tall and strong and handsome, and when she died they lived on happily in the forest, for they did not know their true parentage. Rumi hunted for food in the forest, whilst Rasha kept house and tended their beautiful garden.

One day a royal huntsman stopped at the cottage and asked for a drink. Rumi laid cushions so he might rest in the shade of a flowering tree, and Rasha brought out a glass of pomegranate juice.

"Ah," exclaimed the huntsman in rapture. "This place is almost perfect! If only you had the waters of life, it would be truly paradise!"

Rumi at once resolved that he would find these waters of life and so make their home into a heaven on earth. After the huntsman left, he gave his sister a small sharp knife so that she could defend herself if necessary. Then he kissed her on the cheek and bade her farewell.

"Take care, dear sister," he said. "If I am not back within a month, you will know that something has befallen me. Do not grieve, but make a good life for yourself."

He strode away into the trees, and Rasha waved until he was out of sight. All month she waited, but he did not return. Now, Rasha was a little afraid but she was an enterprising girl. She packed a satchel with some bread and a water-bottle and the little knife. Then she set off to look for her brother.

Rasha travelled eastwards in the same direction that Rumi had done. She walked all day until she came to the edge of the forest. From there she could see white-topped mountains in the distance, and she carried on walking towards them. After a week she came to a place where the path crossed a stream, and there sat a wizened old beggar woman.

"Have you any food to spare?" croaked the crone.

Rasha thought that this would be a good place to eat her own lunch, so she stopped and sat down beside the old woman.

"I've only some dry bread, but you're welcome to share it with me," she answered.

The old woman grabbed the proffered bread and stuffed it into her toothless mouth. It took her a long time to swallow, but at length she spoke again.

"That was kind of you, my dear. More generous than the young man who passed this way last month. He was too busy searching for something to stop. Most unwise, if you ask me."

"That was my brother!" exclaimed Rasha. "Do you know which way he went?"

"He asked me which path to the waters of life," rasped the old woman. "I pointed to the mountains and he went on his way. He would have done better to sit and talk awhile."

"Indeed, mother," replied Rasha politely. "I'm sure you could have told him many things."

"I would have advised him to keep his crumbs," said the old woman tartly. "There's another along the way who would appreciate them."

So Rasha put her last bit of bread back in the bag, and thanked the crone for this advice. Then she set off along the road towards the mountains. After a while, a small silver bird fluttered down towards her. Rasha remembered the old woman's words and took out a handful of crumbs, and the bird perched on her wrist to feed. To her surprise it began to talk in a high melodious voice.

"Pretty girl, why are you going into the mountains?"

"I'm searching for my brother," Rasha replied. "He came this way last month to look for the waters of life."

"Ah, I remember him! Many men have hoped to find that spring, but he was no more successful than all the others."

"What happened to him?" asked Rasha.

"When you seek the waters of life, you must never look backwards. Your brother went up the path and the stones called out, warning him of danger. Because he listened to their voices, he became scared of what lay ahead. He turned around to answer them and was turned to stone himself."

"I will find him and save him," Rasha declared.

She knew that the voices would scare her, so she tore strips of rag from her skirt and stuffed them into her ears. Then, with the silver bird riding on her shoulder, she set off up the mountain. The path wound through boulders, but with the plugs in her ears Rasha could not hear them calling her back. At the top of the mountain she found a sparkling spring which cascaded into a crystal pool. Beside it grew a tree laden with golden apples which hung down over the pond. Rasha was hungry and thirsty after her long climb. She drank her fill of the clear fresh water and cut one apple from the tree. Then she filled her bottle from the spring and set off back along the path. As she went, she sprinkled drops of water on the boulders and they turned back into men. A growing crowd followed her down the mountain, and at the bottom she found that one of them was her brother.

When they got home, Rasha planted her apple core and

overnight it grew into a tree with golden branches where the silver bird perched and sang all day long. Rumi constructed a marble pond and when Rasha emptied in her bottle, the waters of life sprang up in a never-ending fountain.

One day soon after, the Prince Caliph was riding by and his huntsman remembered the beautiful secluded garden. The Prince was so charmed that he returned each day until Rasha agreed to marry him. Rumi came to court and when the Prince succeeded his father, he appointed his brother-in-law as his Vizier. And so the stars turn, and in time everything finds its proper place.

Inspired by a Moroccan story. At the start of this story, Rumi and Rasha embody traditionally male and female qualities. The clever girl must combine the qualities of animus and anima: both courage and kindness are necessary to succeed on this quest. The silver bird represents the spirit, whilst the golden tree is a symbol of wisdom. Together these two watch over the waters of life.

Safe and Sound

Anna, age 3, was playing with her baby brother.
She had squeezed him into one of her old pinafores.
"He's wearing a dress," I observed, trying to hide a smile.
Isn't it so nice when our kids espouse our liberal values?
"Yes," she nodded emphatically. "I've dressed him as a girl, so he won't be stolen by the gypsies."

That's sexism AND racism, then. Wherever did she get it from???
(Note the five finger technique, keeping the story short and to the point.)

Exercise: Show, Not Tell!

This is the first rule for all wordsmiths. It is probably the most important piece of advice you will ever be given. Tattoo it on your knuckles, and your work will immediately improve!

One of the best ways to 'show, not tell' is to provide detail. Give the flower a name: he didn't just give her a bloom; he picked a dead dahlia from someone's front garden, handed it to her with an extravagant bow and ran away giggling.

You can use setting to develop your characters. We judge people by how they present themselves, because we assume that their appearance reflects their inner self. Characters are just the same: their clothes, their actions and their surroundings convey a lot about them. General adjectives are less interesting than detailed description. Supply the specifics which your audience need to know. 'Mary's car was messy' is rather banal. See how this sounds instead:

'Mary opened the passenger door. A drift of sweets wrappers swirled in the sudden draught. She shoved several empty bottles under the mat and threw a blanket into the back seat.

"You can get in now," she said.'

You get a much clearer picture of Mary now, don't you?

In this exercise, you will develop a three-dimensional description for one of your characters. Select someone from your work whom you would like to know better. This should be a major character, or someone who contributes significantly to the storyline. Choose three words or phrases which you feel describe this person.

For example, I might decide that in my story Goldilocks is spoilt; fussy; and careless.

Now think of how you can illustrate these traits using your character's appearance, their actions and their environment.

Goldilocks is spoilt: she has long blonde curls which her mother always brushes.
She is fussy: the first spoonful of porridge was too salty, so she spat it straight out.
She is careless: the little chair broke into pieces which flew all over the floor.

Compose a short piece to describe your character – without using any of the words you selected! Instead, demonstrate their personality through how they look; what they do; and their current circumstances.

Remember that it is much more powerful to 'show, not tell'!

The Good Mother

Mother knows best.

Just Make Do

I didn't feel well this morning.
But I came into work anyway.
You know that old saying:
Children get colds. Men get flu.
Women get on with it.

Humour makes your case more effectively than complaining! (Note the five line structure to keep this anecdote short and to the point.)

Children of the World

Back in the beginning, the Maker lived up above the world in a place that was full of light. It was very beautiful, but he was lonely up there in the brightness all by himself. So he made two little people to live there with him. He fashioned them out of mud and he called them Kwame and Ama. To keep them safe while he was sleeping, he placed a loosely woven basket over the sky. But Kwame and Ama were restless little creatures and they soon got bored. Whilst the Maker was resting, they worked away at one of the holes to get a better look at the world below. And all of a sudden, they tumbled through the opening and landed – bump! – down here on earth.

When they had got their breath back, Kwame and Ama picked themselves up and dusted off the dirt. They looked at each other and they laughed with excitement. They held hands and they skipped off together into the forest. There was so much to see in that new world. Everything was fresh-made and bright-coloured and smelled good. Kwame and Ama wandered around for a long time, sniffing the blossoms and tasting the strange fruits. When they were tired, they lay down under a bush to sleep.

At first, Kwame and Ama were very happy just being together. But after a while, Ama began to feel lonely without their Maker. Lying awake one night, she had an excellent idea.

"Listen," she said to Kwame, "Why don't we make some more little people just like us? We can call them children, and then we'll have someone to care for. I'll shape them out of clay, and you can collect firewood to bake them."

Kwame was very comfortable under his bush: he was quite reluctant to move.

"What's the point?" he said. "If we have little ones, you won't be able to give me all your attention."

"Oh dearest," said Ama cunningly, "If we have children, there will be someone to kick the round ball back to you when I am cooking supper."

Kwame could see the sense of this, so before the day got any hotter he collected a big pile of firewood. Ama shaped small figures out of clay: some boys like Kwame, and some girls like herself. She built a small clay oven and lit a good fire underneath. Then she put the figures in to bake and went to rest with Kwame in the shade.

After a little while she went to take the figures out. They were beautifully brown and when she poked each one in the stomach they were adorably soft.

"That one's done..." she said, "And that one's done..."

When she had checked them all, Ama brought them over to show Kwame. He blew on them to cool them down, and after a while they jumped up and started to run around. Kwame and Ama looked at their small ones, and they were delighted.

But after a while Ama started to get restless.

"I'll make some more," she said. "It seems a waste not to use that oven."

So she made a second set of figures. This time she was impatient and when she took them out they were just golden-yellow. She poked each one in the stomach and they were deliciously soft. Kwame blew cool air on them, and in a moment they stood up and started to chase after the others. Kwame and Ama watched their small ones, and they were pleased. But after a while Ama got up again.

"There's just a bit of clay left," she said.

So she made a third set of figures. There was not much firewood now so she left them in while the oven cooled. When she took them out they were still quite pale, and when she poked each one in the stomach they were quite soft. Kwame blew on them, and they sat up and started to play together. Kwame and Ama looked at their small ones, and were satisfied.

After that, Kwame and Ama were never lonely because they had lots of children to look after. And that's why there are so many different coloured people in the world.

A folk-tale from Ghana in West Africa. In Ghana, everyone is given a name for the weekday when they were born. They have another name too, but their weekday name is important. Kwame is a boy born on a Monday, and Ama is a Monday-born girl.

The Wisdom of Solomon

King Solomon was renowned for his wise judgements. Many difficult disputes were brought for him to resolve.

One day two women were arrested for fighting in the street. They were arguing over a baby, each claiming that the child was hers. Every time the soldiers let them go, the women flew at each other. They screamed and scratched and pulled each other's hair. The women were brought before Solomon and charged with causing a breach of the peace.

Both women told the same story. They lived in the same house, and had given birth within three days of each other.

"She lay on her child in the night, and it died," explained the first woman. "Then she came and took my living babe, replacing it with the body of her own."

"No, indeed," insisted the second woman. "It is she whose child died, and who took my baby in place of hers."

The king listened to this story, and his brow deepened in a frown.

"By rights, you should both be executed for creating such public disturbance," he said. "But I am feeling merciful. Go home, and take the child. Since neither of you has proved a better case, we will have to divide the child between you."

And he told his soldiers to take a sword and cut the infant in two, so that each woman might have a fair half.

The first woman bowed low before the king.

"Noble majesty," she said, "Your wisdom is matched only by your mercy."

And she started to back away from the throne.

But the second woman threw herself sobbing on the floor at the king's feet.

"Great king, I lied," she cried. "The child is not mine. Punish me in any way you see fit. Only spare the life of this innocent child."

Solomon caused the woman to be raised up, and restored the baby to its true mother. But the other woman was taken away and punished according to her crime.

One of the greatest judgements of all time, showing a fine under-standing of human nature. This story is found in the Bible, First Book of Kings, Chapter 3, Verses 16–28.

The Trials of Rhiannon

In the days when kings were greater than they are today, the lord of Dyfed was a man named Pwyll. He was a handsome man and a clever one, and when the time came for him to marry, he found a woman who deserved him. Rhiannon was a fine lady in her own domain. Pwyll first saw her one day when he was making a tour of his distant provinces. The business of court was finished and he set out for his customary evening walk. A woman appeared in the distance riding upon a white horse. Its harness shone with gold pieces and she wore a robe of rich brocade. Intrigued by her demeanour, Pwyll sent a messenger to ask her name. The horse was trotting at a steady pace, but however fast he ran, the man could not catch up with her. The next night the same thing happened, and on the third evening Pwyll himself gave chase. Although the lady's horse never changed speed, he could gain no ground on it until he called out,

"Lady! In the name of love, halt!"

At this, the rider stopped at once and introductions were made. Her name was Rhiannon; she was the daughter of a neighbouring king. As they conversed, Pwyll fell deeply in love with her. The match could not have been more auspicious. His good looks were equalled by her beauty. His pride was balanced by her fine spirits. His wit was matched only by her charm. Pwyll made arrangements to visit her family and their betrothal was agreed. The wedding date was set for a year and a day after they first met.

The marriage was celebrated at her father's house with seven days of feasting. At the end of this time, the happy couple returned to Dyfed together. There was music in the streets when they arrived, and the people showered them with rose petals. Pwyll was a wise and popular ruler, and all seemed set fair for his reign.

But as time went by, a shadow seemed to steal over the land.

Despite her obvious love for her husband, Rhiannon had not borne him any children. The Welsh chieftains were becoming restless. In bars and back streets, it was whispered that Pwyll was not getting any younger. If the king should die without an heir, trouble would descend upon the land. The oldest counsellors had seen such times before. They advised Pwyll that if his wife could not produce a prince, perhaps he should seek another woman who could.

Happily, the longed-for son came at last. The birth was not an easy one: Rhiannon laboured for three days and nights, and her midwives feared that they would lose her. But at last the baby appeared; he was wrapped in a blanket and laid beside his exhausted mother. The waiting-women crept away and let her sleep undisturbed until morning. But when they came at last to wake her, the child was gone.

The women were terrified: surely they would be blamed for this disappearance. Conferring rapidly, they produced a plan. A dog in the courtyard was killed, its blood smeared onto the queen's face. When she awoke, they told her that the baby had not lived. In the madness of grief, she had consumed her own child.

Rhiannon was horrified, but she had no memory to disprove the night's events. The king perforce believed the waiting-women's story. He still loved his wife, but he could not pardon her actions. His court convened to agree a suitable penance for what she had done. It was ordained that since she had acted like an animal, Rhiannon must suffer like a beast of burden. For seven years she must sit outside the town walls, telling her sad story to all who arrived at the gates and offering to carry them up the hill to the castle. All year round, whatever the weather, each visitor to the court witnessed her tearful confession.

This all happened on the eve of May Day, and other strange things came to pass that night. Far away in Gwent, a nobleman called Tiernan was having trouble with horse-thieves. That night he sat up in the stables, for his prize mare had a new foal. Just before sunrise, he saw a huge hairy hand reach through the window. He slashed at it with his sword: there was a dreadful cry, and the hand was snatched away. Tiernan ran outside to give chase, but no-one was there. As he came back into the yard he saw a roll of white cloth lying on the ground. When he unwrapped it there was a tiny boy, sound asleep. He carried the bundle carefully inside to his wife and together they marvelled at the child. From his swaddling he was obviously of good birth, but there was no clue to his parentage. Tiernan and his wife decided to raise the boy as their own.

The child grew quickly, fast as a racing-hound, strong as other boys twice his age. It was clear that he was of noble blood. When he was seven years old, he was already fit to learn the skills of court. About this time the story of Rhiannon reached Gwent. Tiernan saw at once how like Pwyll the boy looked. After some thought, he told his wife of his suspicions. Although she wept, she agreed that they must do what was best for their adopted son. They decided that Tiernan should take him to Dyfed and publicly present him to Pwyll.

It was once more the feast of May Day, and many people had come to join the festivities. Rhiannon met them at the gate, as she did all travellers. She carried the boy on her back up the hill and into the court. The king rose to greet his visitors and invite them to join the feast. Tiernan asked for permission to speak first. He told the story of how he had found the boy. He turned to Rhiannon before the assembled throng and said that she had suffered enough. Would she accept this child as her long-lost son?

Rhiannon stepped forward with the boy in her arms. She looked into his eyes and declared that the child was truly hers. Pwyll came to embrace them, and none could doubt that he was indeed the rightful father. The queen was reinstated to her throne, and the royal couple ruled long and happily together.

This story is related in the great collection of Welsh folktales called the Mabinogion. The Celtic people held horses in high regard, so Rhiannon's trial is not so much a punishment as a form of spiritual purging. She suffers unfairly, but through her sufferings she is elevated to a higher wisdom. It was common for Celtic nobles to send their children to be fostered from the age of seven: note that traditionally boarding schools started at the same age. By this stage it is generally held that a child's moral and spiritual principles are firmly founded. As the Buddhist saying goes, 'Give me a boy for his first seven years and I will give you a man.'

Naomi and Ruth

In Biblical times, there lived a man named Elimelech from Bethlehem in Judah. He went to stay in the country of Moab with his wife Naomi and their two sons. Elimelech died, but the boys married Moabite wives, named Orpah and Ruth. After ten years, both sons also died, and Naomi decided to return to the land of Judah. She said to her daughters-in-law, "Go back each of you to her mother's house." Orpah kissed her mother-in-law and departed; but Ruth wept and clung to her. She said, "Entreat me not to leave you; for where you go, I will go; where you lodge, I will lodge; and your people shall be my people." When Naomi saw that Ruth was determined to follow her, she said no more. So Naomi came to Bethlehem with her daughter-in-law at harvest-time.

Ruth said to Naomi, "Let me go into the field and glean after the reapers." She followed the reapers and gathered the grain they had dropped. This field belonged to Boaz, a wealthy kinsman of Elimelech. Boaz asked his servants, "Who is this?" They replied, "It is the maiden who came back with Naomi from the country of Moab." Boaz approached Ruth and said, "Stay in this field, and keep close to my women. When you are thirsty, go to the vessels and drink." He instructed his young men to leave some grain for her to find, and not to molest or reproach her. So she worked from early morning until evening time; then she beat out what she had gleaned, and went home. Naomi asked Ruth, "Where did you work today?" And when she heard that it was in the field of her kinsman, she was well pleased.

When the harvest was gathered Naomi said to Ruth, "Boaz will winnow the barley tonight. Therefore wash and anoint yourself; put on your best clothes, and go down to the threshing floor. Do not make yourself known to the man until he has finished eating and drinking; but when he lies down, go uncover his feet and lie down there."

When Boaz had eaten and drunk, his heart was merry and he lay down by the heap of grain. Then Ruth came softly, and uncovered his feet, and lay down beside them. At midnight, Boaz awoke and turned over: behold, a woman lay at his feet! He said, "Who are you?" She replied, "I am Ruth, the daughter of Naomi." Boaz said, "Do not fear, for I know that you are a woman of true worth. I am your near kinsman, and I will honour your right."

Next day they arose early, and Boaz filled her cloak with grain for her mother-in-law. Then Boaz took Ruth as his wife, and she bore a boy. Naomi held the child to her bosom, and the neighbour women said, "A son has been born to Naomi."

The Book of Ruth is short, but it is one of the few in the Bible where female characters are significant. This story is about a 'good daughter' as much as a 'good mother', but of course the roles are symbiotic. 'Naomi' means 'pleasant' in Hebrew; 'Ruth' is an older name, meaning 'compassion'.

Exercise: Feel The Love

How do you portray emotion? Love is a many-faceted thing. Passion and jealousy, happiness and sadness are all part of the human condition. The trick is to find something new to say about your experiences.

Think of all the emotional clichés you know:

He could have burst with happiness.
She felt as if her heart would break.
He was green with envy.
... and so on.
These might have been striking images when they were first used. Now they don't seem original, so they are not very effective.

Here is a simple exercise to make your storytelling more vivid. Write your ideas down; if you are working in a group, share them in turn afterwards. You might learn a lot about feelings!

Use your five senses to describe an emotion.
Love looks like...
Love sounds like...
Love smells like...
Love tastes like...
Love feels like...

You can do it for other emotions too.
Hate looks like...
Joy sounds like...
Anger smells like...
Excited tastes like...
Fear feels like...

Which emotion do you find it easiest to portray? What sensory images do you experience most vividly? Why do you think this is?

The Wild Woman

Wild women know they're worth it.

The Selkie

In the north of Scotland, fishermen know that seals are close to human folk. With their big eyes and domed heads, they look like babies – or old men. The seals are fond of music, too. If you sit on the shore and sing to them, they will gather in the water to listen. When there is a full moon, the seal-women come out of the sea. They slide up the beach and shed their silky furs to dance naked on the sand.

The dance of the selkies is not for mortal eyes: the seal-women are shy, and they have memories to mistrust men. There was once a fisherman who longed to see the selkies at play. One evening he crept down to the seashore and hid behind a large rock. It was late summer: the moon hung round and heavy in the sky. The surf broke in silver plumes, and sleek curves glimmered amidst the waves. One after another, seals flipped out of the water to rest on the beach. With a single shrug, they slipped out of their pelts and stood upright on the sand. Transformed into human shape, the girls circled laughing, hand in hand. They did not hear the fisherman tiptoe to the tide-line, seize one sealskin and stuff it into his bag. But they all saw him step out of the shadows towards them. In the flash of an eye the selkies were gone. All but one, who splashed desperately at the water's edge, for without her skin she could not resume her seal shape.

The fisherman took the girl in his arms and tried to comfort her. He promised that he would love and protect her. She cried and pleaded, but he refused to let her go. He carried her home to his house in the village, and swore that she would be his wife. Her sealskin he hid in a wooden chest with a heavy iron lock, to which he had the only key.

The fisherman and his selkie-wife were happy enough over the years. She learned the ways of people, and she bore him three fine sons. Anyone seeing them together could see that she loved her bairns. Yet sometimes, on a stormy night, she would fling open the door and stand staring out towards the sea. At these times the fisherman would take the key in his pocket and go down to drink at the inn, until the mer-lust had passed and she seemed calm again.

One Easter morning, the boys were outside playing when the church bells began to ring. Their father shouted them to come, flung open the great chest and pulled out their Sunday coats. In all the commotion he left the key in the lock. The selkie-wife said nothing, but her eyes gleamed like the sea at sunset. Half-way down the road, she made some excuse and turned back. They were almost at church when the fisherman felt in his pocket and realized what he had done. He ran all the way home, but he was too late: the woman had gone.

Gone, but not forgetting: the seal folk are close to human kind. Each Easter, when the church bells sound, a single seal comes into the bay. It bobs in the water, gazing at the churchgoers with great round eyes. It is the selkie-mother, come to make sure that her children are being properly cared for.

When we take on the roles and responsibilities of mid-life, we often put away our dancing shoes. The trick is always to remember where we keep the key.

Pele's Little Sister

Pele was FURIOUS!

It was not enough that she brought her little sister here in the first place.

Paddling across the open sea with the child tucked under her arm.

How hard do you think it is to manage a boat with one hand?

It wasn't enough that she raised her, fed her, taught her everything she knew.

Gave her clothes when she was cold. Made her shoes when her feet were sore.

Decorated her hair with flowers and sang lullabies to her every evening.

No. This wasn't enough for that bad girl.

She had to have everything her sister had.

EVERYTHING.

There was only one thing that Pele didn't offer to share with her.

One thing – one person – that she loved as much as her little sister.

She saw him in a trance and travelled to his land to court him.

Pele danced for her man like a living flame.

She made the moves that warriors make to signify war.

The woman danced hula to show the heat of passion for her man.

He saw her dance and he loved her: there was no room for any other in his eyes.

When Pele brought her man back to her island, she wanted her little sister to love him.

She wanted them to love each other, so that they could all be happy together on Big Island.

But her sister had to have everything that Pele had: EVERYTHING.

She made fish eyes at the man, and he drowned in her glances.

She spoke sweet words to the prince, and he swooned in her embrace.

One night they stole a canoe and set off for another island.

From the top of her mountain, Pele spied them leaving together.

She knew then that her sister and her man had both betrayed her.

She was ANGRY! Her glare was terrible to behold.

She screamed and shouted at them as they fled.

She threw rocks which splashed into the sea beside their boat.

Only when they were out of sight did she sink down in despair.

Her tears drenched the forest. Her sobs shook the ground.

Her head bowed until her long hair dipped down into the sea.

For many hours she stayed motionless, without a sign of life.

And then she heard them coming back towards her.

The soft splash of a paddle in the waves.

Whispered voices conferring together.

They were returning to her island.

HOW DARE THEY!

Her little sister had stolen her man.

She had been betrayed, deceived, abused.

Did they really expect her to forgive them?

Pele sat up and her eyes glowed red as fire.

Now she was really going to EXPLODE!

Based on a myth from Hawai'i. Pele is the goddess who lives in the volcano on Big Island. Volcanologists have shown how traditional tales encapsulate geological truths. When a volcanic island erupts, it can form a caldera below sea level. Salt water rushes in, and when the cold liquid hits the hot lava it can cause a secondary explosion more powerful than the first. This story conveys the dangers of returning too soon after a volcanic eruption, in a way that is easy to remember.

The Rock Demoness

Once upon a time there was a wise monkey. He lived in the foothills of the Himalayas. Each morning, when he woke, he would sit beneath a certain tree and watch the sun rise. He would meditate on how beautiful the world was, and how lucky he was to live within it.

One day, as he sat deep in contemplation, a demoness happened to pass by. She was a particularly fierce creature, with long black hair and a scarlet face. Moreover, she was possessed of great strength and a terrible temper.

Seeing the monkey lost in thought, the demoness approached with every intention of tormenting him. However, as she crept towards him, a strange thing occurred. Seeing his calm face, the demoness was overcome with a strange passion. She longed to evoke some response from this distant being. Most creatures ran from her, or fell at her feet in terror. The demoness came nearer, and touched his silky fur. Still the blessed monkey did not react. This was a completely new challenge to the wild woman. In no time at all, she had fallen head-over-heels in love with him.

Now, a frustrated demoness is a great danger to the world. In addition, the saintly monkey pitied her frustration and her pain. Eventually, from sheer compassion, he yielded to her entreaties and the relationship was consummated. Then the monkey bade his amour farewell, and went away to continue his meditations undisturbed.

From this union, six children were born. They looked like monkeys, covered in black hair with red faces and tails. The demoness had no experience of being a mother. She herself had been born of the mountain rocks. Consequently she neglected her children, although she loved them dearly. Left alone in the forest, the monkey-children had to fend for themselves. Food was often scarce, and they often fought amongst themselves.

Three years later, the monkey happened to pass that way

again. He was most surprised to see a whole troupe of red-faced children. Because he was an enlightened being, he was not perturbed by their existence. He taught them how to find food, and how to grow grain, and how to comb their hair. He showed them how to tell stories, and propitiate the spirits, and live together in harmony.

Gradually the monkey-children learned to live like proper people. These were the ancestors of human beings.

The people of Tibet trace their descent from this union of the rock demoness with the sacred monkey. She embodies our physical nature; he represents our spiritual side. Our humanity comprises the combination of both these elements.

The Frog Bride

Once there lived a king who had three sons. Now, being king is a tiring job, and the old man wished to enjoy his final years. When the time came for him to retire, he called his sons together.

"One of you will inherit my kingdom," he announced. "Since I cannot choose between you, I will judge you by your wives. A king needs a consort if he is to rule wisely. To ensure you have suitable partners, I have devised some tasks."

Now, the eldest son was already married to a beautiful princess from a nearby kingdom. And the middle son was engaged to the daughter of the wealthiest merchant in the land. But the youngest boy, Ivan, was only fifteen and didn't even have a girlfriend yet. There didn't seem much hope of him becoming the next king. So he fetched his golden football and went to kick it around down by the lake.

He felt so cross that he gave a great thwack! – and the ball flew right across the water. He ran round to the far side, and at first he couldn't find it amongst the reeds. But at last he saw a green frog sitting amongst the rushes holding his ball.

"That's mine," he shouted, rather rudely for a prince. The frog blinked great eyes at him, and to his surprise she spoke.

"Nice to meet you too," she said. "I understand you're in a difficult position. Perhaps I can help."

"You mean my father and the wifely tests? Sorry to sound impolite, but I don't think so."

"At least give me a chance," she said. "Take me home and let me try. Don't worry," she added quickly, as she saw his expression, "You won't have to kiss me."

"But everyone will laugh at me if they see you're a frog!"

"I'll be very discreet," she promised.

Well, there was nothing to lose and besides, she had his golden ball. So Ivan agreed to the frog's proposal, on condition that she stayed well out of sight. That night, he left her in his room nibbling lily leaves whilst he went to the royal supper. When he came back, he was feeling quite disconsolate.

"The first task is to bake a cake," he said. "They are to be judged at a banquet tomorrow."

The frog looked surprisingly cheerful, for an amphibian.

"Leave it to me," she said. "What did you think of the match today?"

And the two of them chatted about sport until the young prince fell asleep.

Next morning, when Ivan awoke, there was the most wonderful cake on his dressing table. It was three layers high, with whipped sugar on top, and it smelled delicious. Ivan carried it carefully to the royal kitchens and gave it to the cook for safekeeping. After dinner that evening, the king called for the cakes. He tasted them all and pronounced Ivan's offering the best.

The older brothers were annoyed, because they knew Ivan didn't have a girlfriend. They hinted that Ivan must have bribed the cook to make a cake for him. Ivan smirked and maintained an irritating silence. After the meal was over he returned to his room, where the frog was sleeping in the sink.

"The next task is harder," he said. You've got to make me a cloak. The court will judge them at the royal ball next week."

The frog grinned at him amiably.

"Don't worry, turnip-head," she said. And they told jokes until the prince began to yawn. All that week, Ivan left the frog resting in his room. Each night they chatted until he fell asleep. On the seventh day, the prince opened his eyes to see a sumptuous cloak hanging on the door. It was made of rich velvet, patterned with gold and jewels. When Ivan entered the great hall that night, everyone gasped with amazement. His older brothers were finely dressed, but Ivan's cloak was magnificent.

His brothers were furious, and accused Ivan of stealing the cloak. Ivan grinned and refused to answer any questions. But when he heard the third task, he knew that the game was up.

"This time we're stuck," he told the frog. "It's a storytelling contest next month. You can't possibly appear in public. My brothers would never let me forget it!"

"Listen," she replied. "Did I ever tell you about the time…"

And she began to relate the most wonderful adventure. That night, and every night for a whole month, Ivan lay awake in the dark and listened to her stories. At last he was convinced that she had a chance, but obviously no-one must see that she was just a frog.

On the night of the competition, a chair was set upon a dais before the crowd. The princess wife spoke first: she retold a tolerable tale that she'd heard from her nursemaid. The merchant's daughter spoke next: she recounted a long story that her father had collected on his travels. When it was Ivan's turn, he asked for a wooden screen to be set across the dais. Moments later, a sweet voice drifted out from behind the partition. The brothers glanced at each other and crept up to the platform. Seizing the screen by both ends, they flung it to the ground.

There, sitting on the chair, was a beautiful girl with green eyes and long golden hair. She winked at Ivan and continued with her story. When she finished, there was a storm of clapping.

Ivan marched up to the dais, took the girl by the hand and dragged her out of sight.

"Okay," he said furiously. "What's all this about?"

"Thanks for being so supportive. I'm under a magic spell, dopey. At midnight I resume my true form, until the first shaft of daylight falls. Then I turn back into a frog."

"And I'm supposed to kiss you, and break the spell?"

"No, actually," she snapped. "Kissing won't work unless I love you. But I could help you rule the kingdom, if you weren't so ashamed of the way I look."

Well, what would you have done?

A modern fairy tale with echoes of many other stories. How many can you identify?

Chang E in the Moon

Yi was a great hero. He was always off fighting monsters, or building castles, or shooting down the sun. This meant that he got lots of praise, and attention, and glittering rewards.

His wife, Chang E, was often lonely. She never got prizes or compliments. She would rather have had her husband to herself. But heroes have to think of their public. Otherwise they would soon lose their popularity.

One day, Chang E was home alone as usual. They had a beautiful house, with wooden eaves and stone floors and painted screens for decoration. Yi was away being heroic, presumably surrounded by crowds of admirers. Chang E had a feeling that he might not be telling her everything about his adventures. She wandered disconsolately from room to room. In one corner, she noticed a wooden box which she had not seen before. Opening it, she found a bundle of silk cloth, and inside a round white pill.

Chang E was curious: holding the pill delicately between two fingers, she touched it with the tip of her tongue.

Just then, the door was flung open. Yi had returned early from his trip. Chang E started guiltily, and the pill fell into her mouth. With an involuntary gulp, she swallowed it.

Now, this pill contained a medicine which made whoever took it immortal. Yi had received it from the Queen Mother in thanks for his services. But the pill was too potent for only one person: he had been keeping it to share with his beloved wife.

Chang E was not prepared for this strong medicine. As Yi watched in alarm, she floated up into the air. She drifted past her husband through the open doorway and rose high into the sky. Up and up she flew, crying helplessly, until at last she bumped into the moon. She managed to catch hold of the hare who lives there, and pull herself to the ground. To this day you may see her sitting there, pounding herbs in the hope of making a medicine that will get her back down. Yi was in despair: he had lost both his wife and his chance for immortality. But the gods took pity on him, and every full moon he is permitted to visit her.

A Chinese story which beautifully encapsulates a common marital situations.

Exercise: Walk This Way!

Some of your characters are wonderful. You like them, admire them, probably empathize with them. Others are less attractive: you've based them on people you don't really like. You hope no-one in the audience will recognize themselves in your work.

At a deeper level, though, each of your characters is your personal creation. They each have a unique set of attributes drawn from your observations of the world. This is what makes your characters come to life: they are based on the perceptions of a real person, yourself. Sometimes you may go beyond personal experience to portray a stronger character. You can do this because the archetypal figures provide a template for developing character. (Archetypes are those outline forms which are innate in the human psyche. They are stereotypes based on common clusters of characteristics. We fill in their detailed appearance on the basis of personal experience.) All of the archetypes are present within each of us, although we may reject and deny them. It follows that all of your characters are potentially aspects of yourself. How else could you know them so intimately? How could you have described them so well? Even your darkest figures emerge from your own imagination. You may dislike them, but you cannot disown your creations.

These darker figures often represent a part of you which you have rejected and suppressed. You disapprove of failings in others that you've managed to avoid yourself. It's galling when guests leave cigarette butts in your flower-pot; annoying when a colleague expects cover for a self-induced hangover; shocking when you see someone hit a whining child. As you read this, feel how you generate energy to criticize and condemn. Today you're going to turn things around and draw on this energy. Stop being prissy: now it's your turn to be the bad one!

When you tell a story, you're conveying your own observations of the world. As a professional it's important that you experience life to the full. So your task today is to do just that – and record it, naturally. Choose a character who you don't identify with, preferably someone of whom you positively disapprove. Next, think of something that they would enjoy doing. This must not involve hurting anyone, but otherwise give your imagination free rein. It can be something small or a life-changing experience. Maybe you'll decide to eat a whole bar of Turkish delight. Or post a letter in your pyjamas. Or go to a bar on your own and start conversations with at least three strangers ("Hello, I'm doing some research for a book..." A good first line helps here!). If you're working with a partner, break physical inhibitions by giving them a foot massage. Or go outside and sing together (especially if you can't sing: tell people you're collecting money for charity). Choose something that makes you feel rather uncomfortable. Otherwise you won't be pushing boundaries, which is the whole point of this exercise. Plan this episode in explicit detail... and do it!

The Grandam

Grandmother, what big eyes you have!

The Seamstress

The hikers had been walking uphill all day. At last the guide stopped outside a small hut.

"We will have refreshments here," he announced. "These villagers are poor but they will give us hospitality. It is a traditional obligation in this area."

The old woman who lived there greeted them warmly. The visitors rested under a tree whilst a small girl brought them drinks and cakes. She was wearing a brightly embroidered dress and one of the hikers commented on this.

"It is made by her grandmother," their guide explained. "She sews all the clothes for her family. It is the custom in this community. The elders sit together and sew while they watch the children. She decorated the dress because she likes to make beautiful things."

"I have a boutique in New York," said the hiker. "I could sell something like that. Ask her if she'd be interested."

So the guide translated this proposal as requested. After a moment's conversation he turned back to the visitor.

"She asks what benefit this would bring her."

"Well, she could make some money," the hiker replied. "This handcrafted stuff sells at a premium. If it goes well, we could expand into more outlets. Maybe develop a mail order business. That way we could make a serious profit. She could buy a house in the city. Employ other women to work for her. Then she could take time off, visit the family, take up a hobby, sit in the sun with her friends..."

The guide explained all these benefits to the old woman, but she just smiled and shook her head.

She's got it all right. 'The Old Fisherman' (The Wise One) is a more concise variant of this story. See how you can take a basic plot and change it to fit your audience?

Give and Take

A man fell into a hole in the road. It was deep and muddy, and he could not climb out alone. Soon a crowd of onlookers gathered trying to help him out.

"Give us your hand," they shouted, jostling eagerly.

But the man stared up at them in shock and would not lift his arm.

Along came a wise woman, a weaver of words. She saw what was happening and made her way to the edge of the hole. Leaning down, she reached out towards the man.

"Here, take my hand," she called encouragingly.

The man reached up and took her hand, and was quickly pulled to safety.

It's not what you say, it's the way that you say it which helps me to hear you.

A Good Woman

Zhen Shi was a master of divination. His advice was much in demand for matters ranging from domestic layout to temple construction. On this particular occasion, he had travelled to a remote area to survey the site for a family tomb. When the consultation was complete, he set off on the long journey home.

It was a hot day and the road was rough. He walked for hours without seeing another human being. His water bottle was empty and his feet ached. Zhen began to fear that he might collapse from thirst. At last he saw a small building in the distance. Nearby, a woman and two boys were winnowing a pile of wheat. Zhen stumbled towards them and the woman came to meet him. She took his arm and led him to the shade of a stunted tree. She picked up a pitcher of water and poured some into a bowl. But before she gave it to Zhen, she stooped and picked up a handful of chaff which she sprinkled on the surface of the water.

Zhen took the bowl but inwardly he was seething. This mark of disrespect was all the more insulting to one as venerable as himself. Before each gulp of water, he had to pause and blow the chaff clear. As he drank, he ruminated on how he could avenge this insult.

"I thank you for your hospitality," he said at last. "Tell me, to whom am I indebted?"

"I am just a poor old woman," she replied. "My husband died three years ago and life is hard. My sons help me to work this farm. By rights they should marry soon, but I cannot afford to feed another mouth."

Zhen was delighted with this response.

"In that case I can help you," he confided. "You will not have guessed from my appearance, but I am a feng shui expert. I can tell you that the source of your problems is the situation of this farm. On my travels today, I passed an empty house which has a very different aspect. It is a little run-down but can easily be repaired. Move there, and your fortunes will definitely change,"

Inwardly he chuckled, for this other house was built in a valley of hungry ghosts. Its site was so inauspicious that it was likely the woman and her sons would die within a year.

Some time later, Zhen happened to be in the same neighbourhood. He recalled the woman and decided to witness his revenge. As he approached, he was surprised to see how rich the valley had become. He passed through fields of crops with many people working there. The tumble-down house had been beautifully restored and was freshly painted. Whilst Zhen stood staring, the door opened and the same woman hurried towards him.

"Oh great master, how can I thank you!" she cried. "Please honour us with your company tonight!"

She led him into the house and seated him ceremoniously at the table. Fine foods and drinks were placed before him, whilst the woman chattered happily about her life.

"It was hard work at first," she confided. "But now everything is going well for us. My elder son is married, and expecting his first child. My younger boy is studying for the government examinations. Thankfully we can now afford to hire help when he is working. And all this good luck is due to your kind advice."

Zhen stirred uncomfortably in his seat.

"I must admit, I am surprised," he said. "I did not envisage this place as fortunate. In fact, when I sent you here, I did not think you would survive."

The woman gazed at him in bewilderment.

"I thought our good fortune was thanks to you. Why would you wish me ill?" she asked.

Zhen was disturbed by her obvious confusion. He spoke defensively.

"I was angry because you had insulted me. I asked you for water, and you sprinkled it with chaff. In revenge I sent you to the worst place I could think of."

"Master, you misunderstood my intentions. When you came to our farm, you were parched. The water in my jug was cold: if you had drunk quickly, it would have been a shock to your system. I sprinkled it with fresh chaff, which you would have to blow away. In this way you paused between mouthfuls and the water revived you."

Faced with such goodness, Zhen could only smile at himself.

"I am humbled by your wisdom. Despite my bad intentions, heaven has favoured you and your family. Your home will undoubtedly continue to be blessed as you deserve."

A Chinese myth. Feng shui is an ancient system which enables people to live harmoniously with their surroundings. Expert practitioners can divine and channel a form of natural energy called 'chi'. Emphasizing the interdependence of people and environment, it combines practical and philosophical approaches to life. But a clever mind is less powerful than a good spirit...

Lucy's Locket

Once there was a girl called Lucy. Her father was a miller, and she lived in a small house beside the river. Her mother died when she was young, so she kept house and looked after her father. Lucy was a sweet, practical, hardworking girl. She wore plain cotton dresses and no jewelry except for a small silver locket. This had belonged to her grandmother, and Lucy always wore it around her neck.

Now, the king of that land had a son who refused to marry. A string of eligible princesses had been brought to meet him, but he dismissed all of them. The king was in despair: he consulted his advisors, and at last issued an ultimatum to his son.

"My boy, you must find a wife," he said. "A ruler must have a consort. If you will not marry a girl of my choosing, find one for yourself. Or I will disinherit you."

Prince Rupert was not pleased to hear this, but he planned to assuage his father's worries.

"Very well," he replied. "I will search for a wife. Just allow me to do it in my own way."

Then he called together his closest companions and asked for their advice.

"By all means, do as your father asks," they counselled. "Invite applicants for the post of queen-in-waiting. But set them a series of impossible tasks. That way, your father cannot say you have opposed him, and you will continue to be able to enjoy the single life."

An edict was accordingly drawn up and posted around the kingdom. But the prince's rudeness was by now notorious, and no suitable candidates applied for the royal hand in marriage.

One spring day the prince rode past the miller's house with his entourage. They stopped by the ford and sent word that his lordship wanted a drink of water. Lucy drew a clean draft and took the cup over herself. The prince was struck by her good looks and easy manner.

His friends noticed this partiality, and decided to play a trick on him. They told the miller that his girl had been selected to apply for the nuptial post. Lucy was reluctant to believe this, but the miller had a high opinion of his daughter. So the following day, he took her to the palace. The miller and his daughter were ushered into the throne room, where the king and prince met each morning to hear the business of the day. The prince was surprised, but not displeased, to see the girl again. However, he had his reputation to think of. So he brought out the list of impossible tasks which he had devised for would-be wives.

"First of all, you must bring me a cherry with no stone."

Lucy curtsied and kept her head down as she left the room, but inside she was seething.

"See, Father? How can I find a cherry that has no stone? He has made a fool of us."

And she ran away and went to sit alone on the banks of the river.

As she sat watching the water, she felt the silver locket around her neck grow warm against her skin. She lifted it up and saw it was glowing very brightly. As she stared, her grandmother's voice spoke to her.

"When the cherry's in the blossom, it has no stone."

Lucy gazed at the locket in disbelief. She got slowly to her feet and made her way back to the mill. The following morning, the miller and his daughter were back at the palace. She was holding a branch of cherry blossom.

The prince was both impressed and disconcerted. He accepted the flowering branch, and posed his next impossible task.

"Now bring me a chicken which has no bone."

Lucy curtsied demurely and left the room. She went straight down to the river, and sat waiting. After a while, she felt the locket starting to heat up. She held it up, and once more she heard her grandmother's voice.

"When the chicken's in the egg, it has no bone."

Lucy ran to the henhouse and searched inside. The following morning, the miller and his daughter were back at the palace. She was holding a warm brown egg.

The prince smiled and accepted the egg. He read out his third impossible task.

"Next, bring me a butterfly that has no wings."

Lucy had solved that one even before she sat down by the river. The locket glowed hotly on her skin. Her grandmother spoke to her:

"Well done, my dear. You have answered all his requirements. Now let your heart be your guide."

The following morning, the miller and his daughter were back at the palace. She was holding a fat green caterpillar.

Prince Rupert smiled thinly, but his voice sounded strained. He was starting to feel trapped.

"Very clever. Now your bonus question: can you bring me a woman who does not nag?"

Lucy looked the prince straight in the eye.

"No, my lord," she said. "I can find one, but I cannot bring her to you. Only a woman without a man does not need to nag."

The prince burst out laughing. "I will accept that for an answer," he said. "You have passed my three tests. You have proved yourself brave and clever and honest. If I must marry, you will do as well as anyone. Will you be my wife?"

Lucy did not answer at once. She felt the locket burn against her breast. Her grandmother's voice echoed in her ear.

"Only if you can solve a riddle for me," she answered slowly. "Tell me a story that has no end."

There was a long silence in the court. At length the prince stood up and stepped down from his dais. He walked towards the miller's daughter and took her hand.

"I will tell you a story that has no end," he replied. "It is the oldest story in the world, and the newest. It goes like this: 'I love you'."

They were married next day amidst great rejoicing and of course lived happily ever after.

Riddling tasks are part of an Old English tradition of oral enter-tainment. Folk songs containing a list of impossible tasks include The Cherry Song; The Elfin Knight; *and* Scarborough Fair (Parsley, Sage, Rosemary and Thyme). *To an audience before books or television, they were a source of amusement and a test of ingenuity.*

All Crazy Now

Matron was a kindly soul and had little time for new-fangled experimentations.

When the young psychiatrist arrived, she summed him up with an experienced eye.

He was obviously newly qualified and keen to apply his years of text-book training.

After the usual delays, the first patient shuffled in for his annual assessment.

"I have a puzzle for you," the doctor announced. "Imagine you have a bath full of water. If I offered you a bucket, a mug and an egg-cup, how could you completely empty the tub?"

The old inmate eyed the expert wearily.

"I'd pull out the plug," he said.

Matron leaned consolingly towards the consultant.

"Shall we see if there's a bed for you?" she suggested.

It takes one to know one, as they say.

World's End

Somewhere on the western side of the prairie, there is a hidden cave. In it lives a woman so old that her face is shrivelled up like a walnut. She is dressed in buffalo skins, the way native people did before white men came. She sits outside her cave, working on a blanket strip for her robe. She is threading it with flattened porcupine quills, the way native people used to decorate their clothes. Resting beside the old woman is a huge black dog which never takes its eyes off her.

A few steps from where she sits, a fire is burning. She lit this fire more than a thousand years ago, and it has been burning ever since. Over the fire hangs a big earthen pot. Inside the pot, berry soup is bubbling. Every so often, the old woman gets up to stir the soup in her pot. She is old and stiff, so it takes her a while to get up and hobble to the fire. The moment her back is turned, the dog jumps up and starts pulling out the porcupine quills. Because of this, the design on her blanket strip is never finished. If she ever completes her work, the world will come to an end.

A Sioux legend recounted to Richard Erdoes. What does this story say to you?

Exercise: Working From Memory

Memory is one of your most important tools, but it is also deeply fallible. When you try to remember something, you may find it hard to recall details; another time you might recollect things which other people contradict. This happens because memory is highly selective. Your mind is a treasure box where you store things that are likely to be important. Later, you can only retrieve things which your brain has bothered to register. To make things even harder, your subconscious mind filters which memories you can access. You tend to remember things which are congruent with your story.

Let's play a game to test your memory. This task is deceptively simple. Try to recall as many small details as you can. Notice how your mind tries to fill in the gaps when you can't remember what actually happened. Is this really what you saw, or rather what you expected to see?

Describe what you saw when you left the house yesterday. What time of day was it? Where were you going? When you stepped outside, what did you see? What was the weather like? How did that make you feel? Who did you meet? What could you hear? What were you thinking about? What else can you remember?

When you've finished, take a reality check. Go outside and see whether the flowers are still there. Ask a friend about their memories of the day. See if you can catch yourself out... or what you could add to the description.

If you need to get your facts right, you may have to supplement memory with research. Whether you're making it up or writing a memoir, accuracy gives your tale credibility. If your villain flees Paris by train, check that he really could get to Rome for midnight. If your heroine grew up in India, let her drink *lassi,* not hot milk. It all makes your story more convincing. A little fact-finding goes a long way!

The Witch

"Come into my parlour..."

Value for Money

It was a very hot day. The tourist was sweating as he wandered around the market place. Finally he found what he wanted. An old Chinese woman sat behind a wonderful array of fans. Big fans; little fans; bamboo fans; paper fans; fans with tassels painted with fabulous scenes, and plain fans with no ornamentation at all. The tourist cracked his knuckles and launched into bargaining mode.

"How much do you want for this?" He pointed to a large decorated fan.

"For you, I make a very good price. Twenty dollars."

"That's extortionate! What about this little one?"

The little old lady was unperturbed.

"My fans are very good price, according to their quality."

"How much? It better be cheap."

"This fan is only six dollars."

"I'll give you five. Here, I pay cash."

"Very good, sir."

The man was gone. But two minutes later he returned, his face redder than ever.

"It's a disgrace! I want my money back! That fan is broken already!"

"How did you use it?" the Chinese woman inquired calmly.

"You fool! I waved it up and down in front of my face, of course."

"That is the answer, sir. With cheap fan, you must hold it very still. Then you wave face up and down before fan."

This is an apocryphal traveller's tale. The old woman in the market-place seems to have cheated the tourist, but ultimately his rudeness highlights his own ignorance.

Pay the Price

A husband and wife had an argument.

She called her mother in tears, and cried,

"I can't bear it any more. I'm coming to live with you."

"No, dear," said her mother. "He must pay for his mistakes...

"... I'm coming to live with you!"

See how the five lines develop this story?

Lost and Found

Once there was a girl who was very beautiful. Her father was dead and she lived with her stepmother on a small farm. Nothing good enough was ever given to that girl. The old woman worked all day long to provide for her family, but the ground was hard and the crops meagre. There was always enough to eat, but never the rich food and sweet spices that the girl craved. Even on feast-days, she would toss her head and turn her nose up at the family fare. The stepmother made all their clothes, but they were not the soft silks and bright satins that the girl longed for. Evidently the crone was jealous of her lovely step-daughter, and she was repaid with spite.

The only person whom the girl loved was her younger sister. This little one looked like some crazy doll. She had round eyes and wild curls and a dark mole on the side of her neck. The older girl would brush her hair and stroke her cheeks, treating her like some small pet animal. Those small gestures of affection were the only sign that the girl had a heart in her chest.

Otherwise she hated her home and spent as little time there as she could. She had an older suitor and plenty of wealthy friends. They all agreed that she deserved a better life than her stepmother would offer her. The day she turned sixteen, the girl had a vicious argument with the old woman. She packed her bag and stormed out of the house, swearing she'd never come back again.

Well, day turns to dusk and white gets dirty. The man married her, and the friends were kind enough, but life in the city wasn't all she'd imagined. She found it hard to get a job without ever having worked a day before. Soon enough she had a baby of her own, and the world closed in around her. Some days she didn't leave the house at all. When her husband came home he'd find her in a dark mood. He started to stay out late, drinking with his mates, and often he'd find somewhere else to spend the night. The bright lights she'd dreamed of were a mocking memory. She carried on because of the baby, but it was hard to remember why she'd ever cared. Eventually the child grew up and went to school, and she got a job as a hairdresser to make ends meet. It wasn't how she'd seen her life turning out, but it felt surprisingly satisfying to bring home money she'd earned herself.

Meanwhile, fortunes had changed back at the farm. Surveyors for a big company had found something under their land. Men in large cars with dark windows came to offer money. The old woman, being as smart as she was selfish, hired herself a lawyer. It turned out that the place was worth a fortune. Enough to buy a smart town house, and take up writing like she'd always dreamed, and send the younger girl to college. That one studied hard, and trained in accounts, and was soon managing a small company of her own.

One day the older girl was doing a lunchtime trim for a businesswoman. As she lifted her client's hair to pin it up, she saw a dark spot on the side of the woman's neck. It reminded her of that little sister and suddenly she felt tears in her eyes. It all came back to her: how happy she'd been before her father died, and her sweet little sister, and her stepmother's face as she slammed the door. She began to talk about her childhood, and it turned out that her client grew up in the same village. It didn't take them long to work out the rest. What goes around comes around, as they say. Here was her own dear sister restored to her. Now she was older herself, her stepmother didn't seem like such a witch after all. And the old woman was delighted to get her first grandchild.

Inspired by a folk-tale from Himachal Pradesh in the Indian Himalayas about a girl who resents the traditional family rituals around the Five Days' Fasting. Like all the best stories, it addresses common experiences and universal themes.

Ceridwen's Cauldron

Long ago there lived a wise witch called Ceridwen. She had one son called Morfran, who was the ugliest child you can imagine. Ceridwen resolved to use her magic arts to compensate for his ill looks. Looking through her books of spells, she found a recipe for a potion that would make him into a wise man. She gathered strange plants and rare herbs, and set her cauldron to boil over the fire. The potion had to brew for a year and a day: at the end of this time, the first three drops would confer supreme wisdom on whoever drank them. For twelve whole months the cauldron simmered, tended by a servant boy called Gwion. On the final day, Ceridwen threw in the last ingredient and lay down to rest. The boy Gwion was stirring the brew when three scalding drops flew out onto his thumb. They were so hot that he stuck his thumb into his mouth to ease the pain. Instantly he was endowed with transcendent wisdom, and the first thing that occurred to him was that Ceridwen would be very cross indeed.

Gwion dropped the ladle and began to run. All too soon, he heard the angry witch chasing after him. Using his new powers, he quickly turned himself into a hare. Swift as thought, Ceridwen transformed into a greyhound and gained on him still faster. He came to a river, and turned himself into a small silver fish. She became an otter, and dived into the water after him. Leaping out, he transformed into a little sparrow. She became a hawk, and sped screeching towards him. Looking down, Gwion saw a heap of grain in a farmyard. He dropped down and turned into a single grain of wheat. Ceridwen turned herself into a hen and began pecking at the pile of wheat until finally she swallowed him.

Ceridwen returned home, still furious at the waste of a year's work. Soon after, she found herself with child, although she had not lain with any man. She realized that the baby must be Gwion, and resolved to kill him forthwith. But when the child was born, he was so beautiful that she could not bring herself to hurt him. Instead, she sewed him into a caul of greased silk and cast him into the river, to let his luck take him where it would.

It was May Day Eve, and downriver a man named Elphin was fishing for the feast. When he pulled in his nets, he found no salmon but instead a small greased bag. He cut it carefully open and to his surprise saw the baby's small bald head inside.

"A shining forehead!" he exclaimed (that is, *tal-iesin* in Welsh).

"Taliesin: that will do nicely," the child replied.

Elphin was so amazed that he nearly dropped the bag, but he took the boy home to his wife and they raised him as their own. When he grew up, Taliesin went to the court of King Arthur and became his chief bard and advisor.

A Celtic story from the great collection known as the Mabinogion. The boy is better known as the wise man Merlin.

Mala

In a small town not far from here, there lived a girl called Mala. Her parents were very poor and she sometimes stole to get food for the family. She dressed in shabby clothes and she often went to bed hungry. One day she was walking through the town when there was a great commotion in the street. People were pushed back and Mala found herself standing at the front of the crowd.

"Make way!" came the cry. "Make way for His Highness!"

The prince rode past, laughing with his friends. The girl looked up into his face and her heart jumped straight onto the saddle in front of him.

Mala went home and that evening she was very quiet. At last her mother noticed and took her aside to talk. The girl would not say what was wrong, for she thought it was a hopeless love. But her mother had been young once and had not forgotten how it felt.

"If you want my advice," she said gently, "Maybe you should visit the old woman who lives in the woods. She is said to be very wise. Perhaps she can help you."

Now, this old woman was widely thought to be a witch. She was skilled in the ways of herbs and medicine, and could mix a cough cure or a poison pastille. She was also said to make love charms, and that was what the girl desired.

So with her mother's blessing, Mala got up early next morning and set off on the road out of town. She came to a junction and took the track that branched towards the forest. She came to the edge of the woods and followed the narrow path that wound between the trees. At length she came to a clearing. A tumbledown cottage stood in the middle of a dirt yard. The shutters swung loose and there were weeds growing through the fence.

"Hello?" she called. "Is anyone here?"

A little old woman came bustling towards her. Her face was

shrivelled and her back was bent, but she was sprightly as a grasshopper. She grabbed the girl by the arm and squeezed hard.

"Aha!" she screeched. "What do you have? What have you come to offer me?"

"I don't have anything to give," stammered the girl. "I've come to ask for something."

"Nothing without something first," the witch cackled. "You seem strong, so you can work for your wish. My poor feet need some rest. Stay here and keep house for me. When you have done enough, you will get what you need."

The old woman seemed strange but not malevolent, so Mala was glad enough to make such a bargain. All afternoon she worked in the house, cleaning the stove and scrubbing the floor. That evening she slept on the floor beside the fire. In the middle of the night she was woken by a horrid scrabbling sound. Standing in the middle of the floor were two enormous rats. Mala jumped to her feet and waved her arms but they advanced, baring their pointed yellow teeth. She seized a broom and brought it down wildly on first one, then the other. Then she swept the bodies outside and sat awake shivering until the sun came up.

When the witch awoke, she seemed quite unperturbed by what had happened.

"Now they won't bother us again," she observed. So Mala pulled herself together and got on with the day's work. When she went to dispose of the rats, it occurred to her that their skins would make supple shoes for the old woman's feet. Overcoming her disgust, she skinned the beasts and pegged the hides in the sun to dry. Over the next weeks she cleaned all day and sewed each evening, and after a month the slippers were done.

The old woman had not spoken much at first, but now she began to talk with the girl. Despite her hooked nose and tattered robe, she was both wise and kind. As they conversed, Mala couldn't help but notice how rough and patched her clothes were. It seemed that the girl was not the only one who could not pay for her heart's desire: being a witch was not a profitable profession. Secretly she resolved to make her a new dress. Around the house grew patches of tall nettles. When she began clearing the yard, Mala cut these down very carefully. They stung her hands a little but she wrapped them in her skirt and carried them to the water barrel. She soaked them for two days and then stripped off the sodden leaves. From the stems she combed fibres longer than the finest linen. These she wove into soft cloth, and after a month she had made a gown fit for a lady.

Now Mala walked with the old woman every day and learnt many things. Spring was turning to summer, and the forest yielded fresh fruits. Mala knew she must leave soon, and she wanted to make sure the house was in order before she went. It was time to clear out the last of the winter stores. In the shed was a barrel of sprouting grain that was no good for human food. Each day Mala spread a little on the ground, and the songbirds fluttered around the yard. At the end of a month, she tipped out the last of the corn and found a silver chain at the bottom of the barrel. She took it to the old woman, who crowed with delight.

"Ah! My old necklace! I wondered where that had gone. It will be my parting gift to you."

And she reached up to fasten the chain around the girl's neck.

"As for those shoes, they are far too fancy for my taste. And that gown is too long for me. You had better have those too."

Mala laughed and embraced her, for she understood now that she had no need of a love potion. She put on the dress and slippers, and danced back through the woods. At the edge of the forest the prince was riding past. He saw the girl standing by the road in her fine gown and soft slippers, and stopped on some pretext to talk. In no time she was sitting up on the pommel of his saddle riding back towards the town. The two were soon married and lived happily together, and Mala was always the apple of the prince's heart.

The name Mala means 'little apple'. The apple tree (genus Malus) originated in Western Asia and was the first tree to be widely cultivated. Apples have been an important winter food in Asia and Europe for thousands of years. The cut cross-section of the fruit forms a pentagram, a shape which occurs in many traditions as a sign of esoteric knowledge. Apples feature in many myths and legends as a symbol for wisdom. In Latin the words for 'apple' and for 'evil' are very similar (mālum, 'an apple'; mălum, 'an evil, a misfortune'). Latin Scriptures probably influenced the apple being seen as the biblical 'forbidden fruit' in the Garden of Eden, and Renaissance painters portrayed this interpretation.

Exercise: Feeling Tenses

Past, present and future: they all have a different effect on your audience. Look at these lines:

He pushed open the door. (Past report)
And it's all dark inside. (Present tension)
And he's about to walk in...! (Future suspense)

Different tenses evoke varying moods, and are appropriate for different kinds of work:

Business speakers and writers usually use the past tense ('This year's results were excellent'). Reports and articles sound more authoritative when they describe completed actions, which is why we refer to the past as the 'perfect' tense.

Novelists generally use the past tense, but they may vary this for impact.

Scriptwriters use the present tense for dialogue and stage directions ('Sam enters the room').

Raconteurs and storytellers often use the imperfect tense ('John was walking down the street...') to create a timeless history. Sometimes they use the present tense, in vernacular speech like street slang, to convey a sense of immediacy ('So he goes to the window, and guess what he sees?').

You can experiment with different time frames to create various effects. For this exercise, take a picture from a magazine showing one or more people. Consider the following questions, and add any more that occur to you.

Where is this scene set?
When is it taking place?
Who is in the picture?
What are they doing?
How do you think they feel?
Why do you think this is happening?

Use your answers to tell someone about your picture... but try experimenting with your time frame. If you are writing, describe what is happening using only the present tense. Re-read your work, but this time translate it into the perfect tense.

If you are talking to a partner, tell them about what has happened using only the past tense.

Note how the time frame affects the mood of your description.

The Noble Youth

He was born with a silver spoon in his mouth.

Good Manners

The young soldier had won a medal for extraordinary courage. The celebratory dinner was a grand occasion. Goblets and glassware crowded along the top table. Files of silver cutlery flanked each place setting. When the first course was cleared away, the head waiter approached the guest of honour. Bowing slightly, he proffered a large crystal bowl.

The steaming water was garnished with refreshing slices of lemon.

The soldier had never seen anything like this before, but it seemed like a nice idea. He took the bowl appreciatively and drank from it.

His face impassive, the waiter retrieved the bowl. With the slightest inclination of his head, the General summoned him over. He lifted the bowl in both hands and took a deep draught. Then he gestured for it to travel on around the table, as a loving cup.

True courtesy is making others feel at ease. By following the soldier's lead, the General shows him real honour.

Prince of Thieves

Hermes was a mischievous child. His father was the mighty Zeus; his mother was a pretty nymph. Being the son of a god meant he had precocious powers. When he was only a few days old, he climbed out of his crib and went exploring. He slipped out of the cave where they lived and wandered through fields and woods. After a while he came upon a herd of cows grazing in a meadow. Without a second's scruple he decided to take them home. He made a willow whip and drove them backwards so their footprints would not betray which way they went.

Those cattle belonged to the sun-god, Apollo (who was incidentally an older son of Zeus). When Apollo found that his cows were gone, he was furious. It didn't take him long to work out what had happened. In a flash he appeared at the mouth of the cave, his face dark with fury.

The infant Hermes was sitting calmly in his crib, burbling to himself. Apollo was not fooled for an instant. He picked up his half-brother by the shoulders and shook him hard.

"Give me back my cattle," he growled.

"Ba-ba," replied Hermes.

"You don't fool me," Apollo snarled. "We're going to talk with Dada."

And he turned towards the mouth of the cave.

Hermes saw that the game was up.

"OK, bro, you win," he said. "Let's not bother Dada. I've got something you might like."

He scrambled back into his crib and produced an odd toy made of cow-gut stretched over a tortoise shell. Smiling sweetly, he strummed on the gut strings and began to sing.

Music tumbled through the dark cave like liquid sunlight.

Apollo had been going to ask where the cow-gut came from; but he was entranced by the sound.

"Give that to me!" he demanded.

"It's for you," cooed Hermes. "It's called a lyre.

"Now you can be the god of music as well as sunshine."

And he looked up at his big brother admiringly.

Apollo was so delighted with his new instrument that he forgave the incident with the cattle.

Hermes acquired a pair of winged sandals, and became the messenger of the gods. He was also the patron of travellers, herdsmen, orators and thieves.

He never risked crossing mighty Apollo again!

Ancient Greek mythology recorded that the gods lived on Mount Olympus. Zeus was the greatest god of the Greek pantheon. He had many sons by different partners.

The Greeks thought that foreigners spoke babbling nonsense: 'Ba-ba' is the root of our word 'barbarians'.

Rama Wins His Bride

King Dasaratha had three wives, but first and fairest was Queen Kaushalya. When she bore him a son, there was great rejoicing in the palace. Young Rama was a handsome boy, beloved by all who knew him. He was good at sport and diligent at his studies. He pleased both the soldiers and scholars at court, for he was both a brave fighter and a wise philosopher. As he grew, it became apparent that his gifts exceeded those of other mortals. His father was glad, for the kingdom would be indeed safe in his hands.

In due course the time came for Rama to seek a wife. Many rajas wished to be allied to this royal house, but the young man desired a wife he could truly love. His heart was stirred by tales of a lovely girl named Sita, daughter of King Janaka of Mithila. She was said to be both beautiful and virtuous, truly a fitting bride for a noble prince. However, winning the hand of such a perfect princess was no easy matter. Faced with many eager suitors, her father had the pleasant task of choosing between them. He therefore decreed a *swayamvara*, or trial of strength, to select a strong and worthy husband. Messengers were sent throughout the land to announce the great assembly. On the appointed day, swarms of hopeful young men gathered in the courtyard, each keen to claim the fair girl as his bride. Among them was Rama with his younger brother Lakshmana, who accompanied him everywhere.

The task which the king set the suitors was to string the Dhanusha, the great Bow of Shiva. The suitors came forward one by one to try, but none could even lift the bow from the ground. There may have been some magic at work here: Sita was said to be the daughter of Bhumi, Mother Earth, and perhaps she was watching to choose a good husband for her child. When Rama's turn came, he stepped up with some trepidation, for he did not know that this was his fate. But the bow seemed almost to leap into his hand, as if greeting an old friend. The assembled court gasped as he flexed the great shaft and strung it easily. Just to prove the point, he let loose a shaft and it flew out of sight. Then he turned towards the royal dais and bowed.

Gladly Sita stood up and took a garland in her hands. She placed it around Rama's neck and smiled at him. The couple were married that afternoon in a shower of marigold petals. After the customary days of feasting they returned to Rama's home in Ayodhya and lived there happily for many years.

But this was just the start of their adventures...

The Ramayana is an ancient Indian epic composed by the legendary sage-poet Valmiki and first written down about 2,000 years ago. Rama has great powers because he has a divine purpose to fulfil. His trials provide an allegory for the journey which each human soul must undertake. Rama's marriage to Sita portrays the perfect union of man and wife; at an Indian wedding, every couple embodies this divine principle. Read 'Rama and Sita' (The Hero) to see what happens next!

The Gordian Knot

When Alexander the Great arrived in the city of Phrygia, he was told of an ancient legend. In the centre of the town stood a temple: in front of this was an old ox-cart. The cart was tied to a post with a rope made of bark, tied in an intricate knot. This ox-cart had belonged to a great king, Gordias: and only his rightful successor could undo the knot.

Alexander stood before the knot and studied it for some time. It was a great mass of matted cords, with no end visible. At length he raised his sword and brought it down sharply, cutting the knot in two. For a moment there was stunned silence. Then the high priest stepped forward and knelt before Alexander, acknowledging him as the true king.

'Cutting the Gordian Knot' is a metaphor for solving an apparently impossible problem by lateral thinking ('thinking outside the box'). Alexander was originally king of Macedonia, in northern Greece. He was a great general and conquered lands across Europe and Asia. When he arrived at Phrygia in 333 BC this action confirmed his legitimate claim to rule.

Theseus' Sword

Do you know the story of Theseus? That's right, the guy who slew the Minotaur. He had help from some girl called Ariadne, but he left her behind afterwards. Cool dude, no strings, looked after number one. It certainly isn't a pretty story. But maybe you don't know why he was so heartless...

Theseus had a tough childhood. Okay, so his mother was a princess. Aethra was her name, and she was said to be a beauty. She lived in a small town called Troezen, where her father Pittheus was in charge. He wanted to put the place on the map: so when Aegeus, king of Athens, was passing through he invited him to a big feast. He got Aegeus drunk and got him into bed with Aethra. Not that he needed much persuasion, for as I've said, she was a pretty girl. Next morning Aegeus was ready to move on, but she pouted and pointed out that there might be consequences of their liaison. Aegeus understandably didn't want to make a commitment at that point, but he realized that this wasn't entirely acceptable behaviour. So he produced an old sword and a pair of sandals, and said that he would leave them for his son. He didn't think it likely that anything would come of this, but just to be on the safe side, he hid them under a heavy boulder. When my son has grown to manhood, he said, tell him to lift this rock and bring these to me as proof of his identity.

Some months later, Aethra did produce a child. To keep things sweet the family put it around that she had also slept with Poseidon, a god with a stormy temper. Quite why having two dads was better than one, Theseus never really understood. But he wasn't one to let the other kids taunt him. By all accounts he was a rough lad, ready to sort things out with his fists when words failed. And if a girl took his fancy he couldn't seem to hear her say 'No'. By the time he was sixteen, Aethra was glad to see the back of him. She showed him where to find the sword and sandals – the leather so damp that one of the straps had rotted off – and sent him off to Athens.

Aegeus never had any other children, so he was happy to claim the boy as his own. But it soon transpired that the lad was trouble. When the chance came to send him off for the Minotaur, everyone was quite relieved. But of course he came back, and his old dad accidentally fell off a cliff, so Theseus became king. He was quite a good ruler, conquered more lands and minted the first money. But he was never popular with the people and eventually he was pushed off a cliff himself. Those who live by the sword must die by the sword, as they say. Such a shame: if only he'd played his cards right, things could have been quite different.

Theseus was raised as a prince, so in his conflict with the Minotaur he is usually portrayed as the epitome of culture overcoming nature. However, his behaviour does not live up to his royal heritage. His later escapades included abducting Antiope, Queen of the Amazons, and kidnapping the infant Helen of Troy. Luckily there was a happy ending for Ariadne: after Theseus abandoned her she was spotted by the god Dionysus and taken to live in the stars.

Blame It On Adam

There was once a boy named Iapo who lived in a small hut on the edge of town. He was very poor, and each day he went into the forest to cut wood. Every afternoon he walked through the streets to the market-place. He called:

"Wood for sale! I must sell my wood! Blame it on Adam! Wood for sale!"

One day the king was passing by and heard the boy's cries. He told his vizier to summon Iapo to him, and asked who had wronged him.

Iapo was overawed but he managed to reply.

"Sire, I have heard that long ago Adam disobeyed God and ate forbidden fruit. If he had not done so, we would all be living in the Garden of Eden and I would not be so poor. That is why I blame Adam for my troubles."

"Hmm," said the king, looking thoughtfully at the woodcutter. "You work hard yet you are still poor. It does not seem fair that you are still suffering for Adam's actions. I am a just man: I will help you."

He ordered his vizier to feed Iapo and give him fresh clothes. That night Iapo slept in the palace on the softest bed he had ever known. Next day the king called Iapo before him again.

"See," he said, "Your luck has changed. Now you will live here in the palace like my son. You may go wherever you like and have whatever you wish, just so long as you never open the green door at the end of the hall. That is the one room you must never enter."

"Oh my lord," cried Iapo, "You are too good! Now I have food, shelter, everything I could wish for. Of course I will never enter the room with the green door."

The weeks passed and Iapo enjoyed his life of luxury. He never had to get up early or work hard; in fact, he even began to grow rather fat. At first he never thought about the room with the green door. But one day he happened to pass it, and began to wonder what lay behind. After that, it began to prey upon his mind. Several times he found himself pausing outside the door. Once he actually laid his hand upon the latch, but he managed to stop himself from lifting it. Still, he could no longer enjoy his leisure so much as he had before.

One morning the king said to Iapo,

"Today I must go to visit another town. I will be gone all day on business. I leave the palace in your hands: please make sure that everything is all right."

Iapo took his responsibilities very seriously. As soon as the king had left, he started a tour of the palace. Eventually he came to the green door at the end of the hall. He stopped outside and looked around.

"I am in charge of the palace," he reasoned. "The king has asked me to ensure that everything is all right. That must include whatever is inside this room. I will just listen to make sure nothing is wrong."

He put his ear to the door, but he could not hear anything. After a few moments, he thought again.

"I am responsible for the entire palace, including this room. I will just look inside to check that everything is all right."

And he opened the door and peered through the crack.

The room was dark and at first he could see nothing. When his eyes adjusted to the gloom, he saw that it was empty apart from a pile of wood and some old rags. As he stared in confusion, a mouse scuttled out and ran past him. Iapo chased it down the corridor, but he was not so agile as he used to be. He tripped over his fancy robes and the mouse escaped.

He lay on the ground sobbing and heard the king's voice.

"Why are you lying here in disarray? I left you in charge of my palace. This is not a seemly way for a prince to behave."

Iapo was confused, guilty, terrified.

"My lord, I am so sorry," he gasped. "I have let your mouse escape. I did not mean to lose it. I will find you another."

"My mouse? What mouse?" asked the king.

"The one you keep in the room with the green door. He was so fast, and I did not know..."

The king spoke in sorrow more than anger.

"I see," he said. "So you have opened the green door. The one thing that I forbade, you have done."

He turned to his vizier.

"Take him to the room with the green door," he instructed. "Return his rags and his wood. Let him go back to the life he had before. Now he knows that no-one else is responsible for his fate."

So Iapo went back to his hut on the edge of the village. Every morning he went to the forest to cut wood, and every afternoon he took it to the market-place. He shouted,

"Wood for sale! I must sell my wood! Come and buy fresh firewood!"

But he no longer said anything about Adam.

A Nigerian folktale about taking responsibility for your own situation. Iyapo is a Yoruba word meaning 'Troubles'.

Exercise: Avoiding Adjectives

Remember that great adage 'Show, not tell'? It's time for some more practice on that front. Today you are going to confront one of your greatest adversaries: the adjective.

Ah yes, those little 'describing words' are anarchists in disguise. They lurk waiting to make the storyteller look ridiculous. They sabotage plenty of perfectly respectable writing.

"Andy was a tall, thin man with a long, straggly beard. He had a small ginger cat, which loved to eat smelly old sardines. One wet winter morning, Andy and his cat saw that the battered wooden cupboard in their shabby little kitchen was completely empty..."

Not one of my best pieces of work!*

So for this exercise you are going to shun the 'a'-words. No adjectives, and none of their subversive cousins the adverbs. The hero doesn't need to rush quickly, if he was rushing anyway.

Like any prince, you have to engage in single combat. All that you get here is your starting line. You're going to describe a scene: you can decide where it is, what is actually happening, who is watching, what their thoughts and feelings are. You can even decide whether you're looking out or in. The only constraint is that your first sentence must begin with these words:

"Through the window..."

*Of course, the extended adjective list can be very effective if used deliberately. "In a deep dark cavern, in a cold damp valley, on a high distant mountain, there lived... a mouse!"

The Urchin

Learn to paddle your own canoe.

Bad Boy

Billy is always getting into trouble.
Today he pushed to the front of the lunch queue.
The other boys shoved him back and they got into a fight.
His big brother saw what was happening, and shouted:
"DON'T HIT MY BROTHER!
"...Let ME do it!"

LOL! That's Laugh Out Loud (or 'lots of love', depending on your age).
The five point structure has a codicil here!

Slowing Down the Sun

In the beginning, the sun was much younger than he is today.
Like any youth, he was hot and fierce and fast-moving. Each day
he leaped up and raced across the sky as quickly as he could.
Then he would lie down on a pile of clouds and rest until
morning.

This was not good for the people down on earth. The days
were too short for the men to do their farming and fishing. There
was not enough time for the women to sew clothes and cook
food. Worst of all, it always got dark before the children had
finished their games.

"Please, let us play a little longer," they cried, but their
mothers always answered, "No! Your shadow has gone to sleep,
and so must you."

One day Maui, the boy hero, decided that he was going to do
something about this.

He called his brothers together and made them promise to do whatever he said. (When you have a hero brother, it's best to go along with whatever he wants.)

Maui showed them how to twist long ropes out of plant fibres, like the men did to make fishing nets. At the end of each rope, he made a loop. Then he led his brothers to the top of a high hill, just below where the sun came up each day.

Next morning when the sun rose, the brothers threw their lassoes around him. The sun laughed at this new game. He rose fast, slipping through each rope as it landed. Soaring up into the air, he turned and dived to the western horizon. That day was shorter than ever, and the people wept with frustration. The brothers looked at their charred ropes and they were sad. But Maui was not disheartened.

"We have learned that this is not enough. Next time, we will make better," he said.

The brothers twisted fibres into fresh ropes. They took several ropes and spun them together, to make one thick strand. They made a noose in this and waited below the brow of the hill.

As the sun rose, they threw the rope around him.

The sun frowned at this new challenge. He struggled furiously and slipped through the noose. Blazing with anger, he rose high into the sky. That day was hotter than any had ever been. The brothers looked at the great noose and they were sad. But Maui was not discouraged.

"We have learned that this is not enough. Next time, we will pull together," he said.

So the brothers went to work once more, and this time they made many thick ropes and wove them into a great net. They waited below the brow of the hill and as the sun rose, they threw the net over him.

The sun fought furiously, but he could not break through the many strands. The brothers held him pinned to the ground until at last he gave up and asked sulkily what they wanted.

"It is this," said Maui. "Every day, you race too fast through the sky. We will let you go if you promise to slow down. Then people will have long enough to do their work. And children everywhere will love you, because they can play for as long as they can see their shadows."

The sun could see that he had no choice, so he agreed and the brothers released him from their net. The sun rose slowly and sulkily, but when he saw how happily the people looked at him, he decided that it was not such a bad deal after all. The only problem was the mothers, because they had not been told about their side of the bargain. They don't realize that children should still be allowed to play all day, so long as they can see their shadows.

A favourite myth from the Maori people of New Zealand. The Urchin is often portrayed as a junior version of the Trickster.

Monkey Business

Alan was very fond of his camera. A digital Nikon, it had travelled with him across Indonesia. A whole month of his life was stored in that photo stream.

The big macaque seemed keen to feature in his story. It sidled close and posed obligingly. Alan raised his camera and focussed on the image. Suddenly the monkey swung towards him. It grabbed the camera and leapt into a tree. From the branches it peered down at him, chattering crossly.

"Dammit!" Alan shouted. "Give that back to me!"

But the monkey did not appear to understand.

A small boy tugged at Alan's sleeve.

"Sir, I can help. Give me ten dollars."

"Go away!" cried Alan crossly, but the boy was unperturbed.

"You give me ten dollars and I get your camera back."

Anything seemed worth a try. Alan produced a crumpled

note, and the boy ran off. He came back moments later with a small bag of peanuts and grinned at Alan.

The boy and the monkey exchanged looks. Then the boy began throwing peanuts up to the macaque. He caught them neatly with a practised hand. The camera dangled precariously from his other paw.

"Why are you feeding him?" demanded Alan, but the boy ignored him.

When the monkey's paws were full, the boy tossed up one last peanut. As it curved through the air, the monkey made his choice. Dropping the camera, he caught the peanut and made off. The boy retrieved the camera and handed it solemnly back.

Uluwatu Temple in southern Bali is a popular tourist destination. It is famous for its resident troupe of macaques. The monkeys might look cute but actually they are a menace. Expert thieves, they tithe the tourists like professionals. This is how they work…

King of the Birds

One day the birds were chattering together and they began to argue. Which bird was the best? Who should be king of them all? How could they choose? So they decided to hold a competition. Since they were all birds, naturally what they could do best was fly. And biggest – or in this case highest – is obviously best. Whoever could fly the highest could rightly claim to be king of the birds.

So they all lined up together and launched off into the air. The ostrich didn't get very far, of course. The parrots flew a bit higher, but they got distracted by some trees. The pigeons took cover as soon as they could, and the kestrels had a habit of hovering. But the great eagle soared high up into the sky, until everyone's eyes were so dazzled by the sun that they could hardly see him. When all the other birds had landed he started to descend in great spiralling arcs, and he landed majestically upon the ground. The other birds gathered round respectfully as he preened his feathers.

"So are we unanimous?" he enquired, and the feathered flock chirped their respectful adulation.

Except one.

Suddenly there was a stir on the eagle's back. A small brown sparrow hopped down from where he had hitched a lift.

"Excuse me," he said, "But I think you'll find that technically, I went higher."

And so it was through guile that the sparrow won the title, 'King of the Birds'.

It's always satisfying when the small one wins!

Mirror Mirror

There once lived a barber who was very poor. The fashion in those days was for men to wear their beards long and their hair untrimmed. The poor barber tried to tempt customers into his shop with offers of tea and foot massage, but alas, the townsfolk were immune to his connivings. At last he decided to close his shop and try his luck in another place.

He packed a small bag and the following morning he set off. He walked all day until he came to a village. There he found lodging for the night, but no-one who wanted a barber to cut their hair or beard. The next day he travelled further, and the next, and the next, but wherever he went the answer was always the same: "No thanks." "No thanks." "No hairdressing here."

As he walked further from the city, the farms became less frequent and the villages further apart. At last there came an evening when there was no house in sight. The barber resigned himself to a night in the wilderness. He made a bed of leaves under a spreading tree and settled down to sleep.

Now, this tree was the home of a fierce werewolf who was not happy to have company. When he heard the barber's snores, he leapt down and started kicking furiously at the leaves. The barber was awake in a flash and jumped to his feet, the hair on his head standing up like a badger bristle brush.

"A-hah!" cried the werewolf. "So you dare to invade my space! Well, I'm grateful when my supper delivers itself. Run if you like, I prefer fast food."

The barber was shaking so hard he could hardly speak, but he was thinking quickly.

"My dear sir," he stuttered, "Surely you don't think I came here by accident."

The werewolf paused for a fraction of a second: his curiosity was piqued.

"What do you mean?" he snarled. "Don't think you can fool me, man!"

"Obviously I've come to help," explained the barber, more suavely now. "Have you seen yourself lately? Fashions are changing in the town, you know." Bending down to his bag, he took out the hand mirror that he gave his customers to hold.

"Do you think I care how I look?" muttered the wolf. But he could not resist glancing at his own reflection. And once he had glimpsed himself, he wanted a closer look. He took the mirror and examined himself, turning this way and that.

"You see, sir," extemporized the barber, "Hair is worn neater now. If sir would just lift the fur from the nape of his neck... And push back the sideburns... You see how the shape of the face shows better. If sir will permit me, it will be a most flattering cut."

Well, the werewolf was not used to such attentions, and in no time at all he was sitting on a stump wearing a white robe with his fur covered in shaving foam. The barber did consider cutting his throat, but professional pride made him want to complete the job. When he had finished, the werewolf looked quite civilized.

He held the hand mirror to one side and then the other, primping and posing like photoshoot.

"You know, I rather like it," he observed. "Perhaps I won't eat you after all. It would be a shame not to be able to maintain this look."

The barber felt relieved, and also rather thoughtful. Although werewolves had not been his traditional market, there were obviously opportunities here for the entrepreneuring stylist. He resolved at once to investigate this new market. When he came to the next town, he set up shop in the market place offering haircuts to anyone and everything. Soon he could afford a shop of his own, with separate entrances for every class of customer: boys and teenagers, dogs and pet sheep... and of course werewolves.

Problems are just opportunities in wolves' clothing.

Vice Versa

Gerry was the coolest boy in school. His tie was always knotted a fraction looser than the other lads, his belt slung suggestively lower. His long fringe flopped on the borders of respectability. He would have been in constant trouble if he had not made the teachers laugh.

The boys used to skip lessons and sneak off to smoke behind the library. One day Gerry was caught skulking there and sent to see the headmaster. His friends hung around outside to hear the verdict. To their surprise, Gerry sauntered up smiling.

"No problem. I can go there any time during study periods."

"But surely it's against school rules!" the others protested disbelievingly.

"Smoking, yes... but I explained that when I'm working in the library, I sometimes need a breath of fresh air."

It all depends on how you present things...

Scarface

Once there lived a Blackfoot chief who had a very beautiful daughter. Many men wished to marry her, but she refused them all.

"Why should I take a husband?" she said. "My parents take good care of me. Our lodge is large, our blankets warm, our pots always full of food. I am happy as I am."

After she had turned down every suitor, her father became angry, and her mother anxious.

"We will not be here for ever," her mother said. "It is right that you should find your man."

"Listen," she told them. "The Sun has told me not to marry. He says I must await his favour if I wish to have a happy life."

"Ah," her father said, "It must be as he decrees." And they spoke no more about it.

There was one boy who had not dared to ask. He was an orphan: the women of the tribe had raised him and the men taught him hunting. One day the boy was alone in the forest when he came across a bear. He wrestled with it and drove it away, but its claws raked across his cheek leaving a long red mark. After that, he was known as Scarface, and the other boys laughed at him.

"She has turned us all down. Why don't you ask her to marry you?" they teased. "How could she refuse one so handsome as you?"

Because he loved her in his heart, Scarface determined to do as they suggested. He went and waited by the river. After a while the girl came to fetch water, and he approached her. He told her of his love, and how he longed to marry her. At first she hid her face in her robe, but after a time she spoke.

"I have refused many men, yet I am honoured by your words.

You are poor, but my family have enough for both of us. You have shown that you are strong: the story is written on your face. There is only one obstacle to our union. The Sun has told me that I belong to him. You must go and ask his favour."

Scarface was dismayed, but he decided to search for the Sun's lodge. For many days he travelled: he crossed great plains, and climbed high mountains, and followed rushing rivers. Often he lost the trail, but the animals of the forest guided him on his way. At last he came to the edge of a great water. It was so wide that he could not see the other side. He sat down in despair, but the birds took pity on him, and carried him to the other side. Here a path led upwards, and Scarface set off along it. After a while he came across a fine bow and arrows by the side of the path, but he left them where they lay. A little farther on he met a boy, handsome though strangely dressed, his clothes decorated with bright feathers. The boy spoke to him, and asked:

"Have you seen some weapons on your way here?"

"Yes," answered Scarface. "I saw a bow and quiver lying by the path below. I left them for their owner to return."

"You are honest," observed the boy. "I am glad to have them back. Who are you, and where are you going?"

Scarface explained his journey, and the boy exclaimed,

"Why, the Sun is my father! I am Morning Star, and my mother is the Moon. Our lodge is nearby: you will be very welcome."

Scarface was received kindly by the family and stayed for several days. Morning Star was glad to have a companion, for he usually had to play alone. One day they went hunting down beside the big water. Morning Star ran ahead, and disturbed a flock of huge fierce birds. Scarface sheltered him from the birds' attack, spearing one after another until they all lay dead. When she heard the story, Moon wept and thanked him for saving her boy's life. Sun was equally grateful upon his return that night.

"You are brave," he said to Scarface. "I would like to reward your courage. Tell me what I can do for you."

"There is a girl whom I would like to marry," said Scarface. "I asked and she was glad, but she says that she belongs to you. She told me that I must ask you for her hand."

"She is wise to heed me," said Sun. "She will be happy and live a long life. Now I give her to you gladly, for you are strong and honest and brave." He touched Scarface's cheek and the red mark disappeared. Then he took him to the edge of the sky and showed him the short trail home, the Wolf Path which we know as the Milky Way.

Early one morning the people saw a stranger approaching their village. He wore fine clothes and carried strange weapons. They knew his face, but it was not the face they had seen before.

"The scar-face boy has returned. He is no longer poor. The mark on his face is gone," they cried in wonder.

The beautiful girl came out and stood by her parents' lodge. The handsome young man came up to her.

"The trail was long," he said. "I nearly died, but the animals helped me along the way. The Sun is happy for you to be my wife."

The girl was glad to see him return. They were married with great rejoicing, and the Sun shone on their union.

A Native American parable about finding your own way in life.

Exercise: What's In My Pocket?*

This is another way to practise engaging all your senses fully in your descriptions.

Take an object which you regularly carry in your pocket, handbag or briefcase. It might be a keyring, a wallet, a good-luck charm... Write a short poem about this object, with one line for each of the five senses. Use the most imaginative similarities and metaphors you can find. Remember that 'a poet is someone who can see connections which no-one else has seen'. A metaphor literally changes an object into something else in your mind, through a process of metamorphosis.

When I hold this, it feels like...
When I regard this, it looks like...
When I shake / hit this, it sounds like...
When I lick this, it tastes like...
When I sniff this, it smells like...

If you are working with a partner, see if they can guess what this is from this description.

Finally, write a sixth line describing its function, or saying what your object does.

*"What have I got in my pocket?" This is the question which Bilbo Baggins, the Hobbit, famously asked Gollum.
(Answer: A magic ring.)

The Hero

Who dares, wins.

Lifting the Sky

When the Great Spirit first made the world, he began in the east and walked westward, creating as he came. He made people as he came, and to each group he gave a language so that they could talk together. But the groups could not talk to one another, and this made it difficult to communicate.

The world in those days was a beautiful place, but it had one problem. The sky was so low that tall people constantly bumped their heads against it. Sometimes boys would climb trees and actually walk upon the sky, and this was very dangerous.

At last everyone decided that something must be done. The leaders of all the tribes met together and devised a plan. They agreed that all the people of the world must unite to push the sky higher up.

"We can do it if everyone pushes at the same time," said one. "All the people, and all the birds, and all the wild animals."

"But we have never worked together," objected another. "We don't all speak the same language. How will everyone know when to push?"

"It is simple," said a third man. "We will make a new word that means the same for everyone. When we are ready to lift, let someone shout 'Ya-Hoh'! That will mean 'Work Together' in all our languages."

So the council sent messages to all the people of the world, and all the birds, and all the animals, telling them that they were going to lift the sky. The people made poles from tall fir trees and the birds preened their feathers in readiness. On the appointed day, all the people lifted their poles and stood ready to push.

Then the leaders shouted, "Yah-Hoh!" Everyone pushed, and the sky shifted a little. They shouted, "Yah-Hoh!" again, and the sky moved up a little more. With each shout everyone pushed as hard as they could, and the sky moved until it was in the place where you see it now. Since then, no-one has bumped their head against it, and the boys cannot climb and play upon the sky. Only the spirits rise up to that place, and at night we see their campfires as stars in the sky.

We can still shout, "Ya-Hoh!" when we need to work together. As we say that long "Hooooh!" we use all the strength we have. When we all work hard and encourage each other, we can achieve whatever we want.

A Native American story. The Snohomish people lived in tiny groups scattered across what is now western Washington State. This tale teaches the value of cooperation.

Rama and Sita

One day, Prince Rama and his brother Lakshmana decided to go hunting. Rama's beautiful wife Sita accompanied them to the forest. They left her sitting in a clearing and went to see what the day would bring. What the day brought was a demoness, out gathering flowers. She was very taken with the handsome young prince, and wooed him with words of love. Rama and his brother were insulted: did she really imagine that he would ever look at one so ugly as herself? They responded to her overtures with jeers and scornful blows. The unfortunate demoness fled in floods of tears, calling upon her brother for revenge.

The demon Ravanna responded to his sister's pleas. Mounting his flying chariot, he swept into the air. He hovered above over the trees, searching the cause of his sister's distress. Sitting in a clearing on the banks of a stream he spied Sita. Her face was radiant as the summer sun. So gentle was her voice that the wild animals lay peacefully around listening to her sing. Ravanna's heart was smitten and all thoughts of vengeance left his mind. Like a thunderbolt he swooped down, seized her by the waist and pulled her into the chariot. Sita screamed but it was impossible for her to resist him. The great eagle heard her voice: on mighty wings he flew after the chariot and seized Sita's belt but Ravanna beat him off. The eagle fell to the ground with a fragment of the golden riband in his claws.

Rama returned home many hours later, singing jubilantly after a successful hunt. When he found Sita gone, he was filled with rage and despair. He searched the forest and at last came upon the eagle, still clutching the golden belt. The dying bird whispered the tale of what he had seen. Rama's spirit was restored and he resolved at once to search for Sita. He set off southward, in the direction which the bird reported the demon had flown.

After many days Rama came across a tribe of monkeys. They chattered and teased him, but at length they took him to their leader. Hanuman, the Monkey General, was touched by Rama's story and agreed to help search for the missing girl. From Rama's description he recognized the aerial abductor as the Lord of Lanka, an island to the south-east of India. Hanuman rallied a huge army of monkeys and set off with Rama towards the nearest point on the mainland. The General realized that if they ventured the crossing in a fleet of boats, they would be an easy target for Ravanna's troops. Accordingly, he instructed each monkey to find a large stone on their journey and carry it until they arrived at the edge of the sea. When they reached the shore opposite Lanka, each monkey hurled his boulder into the water. They were so many that the stones rose up and formed a narrow causeway. Swarming across, the monkey army laid siege to the demon's fortress.

Meanwhile, Ravanna had behaved with surprisingly solic-itude towards Sita. He did not wish to ravish her, but rather to win her love willingly. Accordingly he placed her in a fair garden surrounded by attendants where he visited her daily, soliciting her affection. However, Sita was as loyal as she was fair: she therefore retained a virtuous demeanour, nor gave Ravanna any grounds to hope that his suit would ever be successful. She was certain that Rama would come for her, and constantly repudiated her captor's advances. Eventually even the noble demon's patience began to wear thin. He declared that he would give her one more week: at the end of this time, it would be a year since she had become his guest, and if she would not cede willingly then he would take her by force.

Sitting beneath a flowering tree, Sita heard the noise of battle and knew that her faith had been justified. From the walls of the fortress, devil soldiers fired blazing arrows but the monkeys surged forward in relentless waves. At length the great doors opened and Ravanna himself sallied forth. His hands were filled with weapons and his appearance was terrible to behold. The monkeys fell back but Rama himself stepped forward and challenged the demon to single combat. The pair fought ferociously: first one appeared to be gaining ground, then they would stumble back the other way. At sunrise on the third day, Rama finally dealt his opponent a mortal blow in the chest. Ravanna fell to the ground and his forces melted away around him. Rama then gave a great speech celebrating his victory but proclaiming Ravanna a worthy opponent whom he was proud to have overcome. Meanwhile, Hanuman found the garden where Sita was waiting and escorted the princess back to her lord.

The Ramayana is one of the best-loved stories in the world. It is known across India and South-East Asia. Diwali, the autumn Festival of Lights, celebrates the return home of Rama and Sita. In Indonesia, the wayang purwa shadow puppets relate their adventures; in Thailand, the king explicitly models himself upon Rama as the ideal ruler.

In this story there are actually three heroes. Rama's courage symbolizes the indomitable human spirit. Hanuman's cunning stands for our mind, or restless intellect. The demon Ravanna represents our physical body, whose desires must be subdued if we are to gain enlightenment. As Rama's final speech indicates, all three aspects of the Self play a vital part in our life stories.

Sharpen the Axe

A few years ago, the World Logging Championships were held in Quebec. The rules of the competition were simple. Each contestant was given an area of pine forest. Whoever cut the most timber in one day would be declared the winner.

The two favourites were a Canadian and a Swede, and they were allocated adjacent plots. When the starting whistle blew, they both began to chop at the same steady pace. The sound of axe blows echoed through the forest. After an hour, the Canadian paused for a quick drink of water. He was pleased to hear his opponent stop too and take a longer break. After several minutes the thudding started again, and the two men swung in rhythm for a while. An hour later the Canadian took another swig of water, and once more the Swede stopped for longer. Sensing his opponent's weakness, the Canadian returned to his work with renewed vigour. And so it continued all day: each hour the Canadian only paused for a quick drink while the Swede took several minutes' break. When the final whistle sounded, the Canadian was confident that he had won.

However, when the logs were counted, the Swede was declared the champion. The Canadian managed to smile as they shook hands, but he shook his head in disbelief.

"How did you do it?" he asked. "I could hear you cutting, and every hour you rested. We must have been matching blow for blow. I don't understand how you felled so much more than me."

"My friend, it's simple," replied the Swede. "Every hour you stopped for water. I sharpened my axe."

Preparations for the task are just as important as the effort actually expended.

Perseus the Petrifier

King Acrisius of Argos was warned by an oracle that his grandson would kill him. Since he had only one child, a daughter named Danae, Acrisius imprisoned her in a dungeon guarded by savage dogs. Unfortunately Danae was a pretty girl, and had caught the eye of the great god Zeus. He came to her in a shower of gold and begot upon her a son named Perseus. When Acrisius learned of the child's birth, he dared not kill his daughter. Instead he put her and the child into a wooden chest which he cast into the sea. They drifted to the island of Seriphos, where they were found by a fisherman who took them into his own house. There Perseus grew to manhood, strong and clever and skilled in many things.

One day the king of the island was passing by and saw Danae sitting by the shore mending nets. He was struck by her beauty, but Danae rejected his advances. He tried to take her by force, but Perseus heard her cries and came running to defend her. King Dictys was shamed and furious: he determined to dispose of this brash young man. Returning to his palace, he sent out messengers to proclaim his forthcoming wedding to a foreign princess. Every man on the island was commanded to contribute one horse to the bride-gift. Perseus did not have a horse to give, but rashly promised to contribute anything that could be obtained with courage rather than cash. This was exactly what the conniving king had hoped for. Gleefully he specified his price: the head of the Gorgon Medusa.

The Gorgons were three monstrous sisters with serpents for hair, brazen claws and such terrible faces that all who gazed upon them were petrified: not just afraid, but literally turned to stone. To approach them was effectively to court certain death. Fortunately, Perseus' prowess had also attracted the attention of a deity. Athene was the goddess of wisdom and warriors: manifesting in a flash of light, she proposed to help Perseus with his quest.

The trick, Athene told him, was never to look at Medusa directly. If he only saw her reflection he would be safe from her lethal gaze. She presented Perseus with a polished shield which he could use as a mirror. She also lent him an adamantine sickle of great sharpness; a pair of winged sandals from Hermes; and a helmet of invisibility belonging to Hades, lord of the underworld. Perseus performed exactly as the goddess had instructed. Wearing the sandals and helmet, he approached the awful sisters when they were asleep. Using the image in his shield to guide him, he struck off Medusa's head and swiftly flew away.

On his way home, Perseus spotted a beautiful girl chained to the base of a sea-cliff. Her charms were made more obvious by the fact that she was stark naked. Fluttering down, Perseus tried to engage her in conversation. Between sobs she explained that her name was Andromeda and she was being sacrificed. It was all the fault of her mother, who had boasted that she was fairer than a mermaid. Poseidon, god of the sea, was enraged and sent a vile serpent which only daily meals of maiden could placate.

Perseus' duty as a roaming hero was obvious. He lurked behind a rock until the monster emerged, then stuck out Medusa's head. The serpent was turned to stone, its coils protruding from the water as a line of rocks. Some sea-weed was accidentally transformed too, and formed the brittle twigs now known as coral. Andromeda's parents were suitably grateful for being released from this terrible trial. Ignoring the girl's previous engagement they quickly betrothed her to Perseus, who took her back to Seriphos.

King Dictys had been quite complacent about his prospects

with Danae. Her son's return was a most unwelcome surprise. The shock was short-lived: Perseus showed his trophy and transformed him into a statue. The young champion then set off for Argos to visit his natal home. Perseus accidentally killed his grandfather at a discus competition, and thus the prophecy was fulfilled. Whether it's nature or nurture, none can tamper with fate.

This is one of the great hero myths from Ancient Greece. Perseus' story tells us that we don't have to accept our lot in life. However, it is vital to act with a good heart. The end cannot justify the means: in trying to avert the prophecy, Acrisius actually brings it to pass. For another example of this, see 'An Appointment' in the Ogre stories.

Tom Saves Becky

Mr Dobbins had reached middle age with an unsatisfied ambition. The darling of his desires was to be a doctor, but poverty had decreed that he should be nothing higher than a village schoolmaster. Every day he took a mysterious book out of his desk and absorbed himself in it at times when no classes were reciting. He kept that book under lock and key. Every boy and girl had a theory about the nature of that book; but there was no way of getting at the facts in the case. Now, as Becky was passing by the desk, she noticed that the key was in the lock! It was a precious moment. She glanced around; found herself alone, and the next instant she had the book in her hands. The title-page – Professor Somebody's 'Anatomy' – carried no information to her mind; so she began to turn the leaves. She came at once upon a handsomely engraved and coloured frontispiece – a human figure, stark naked.

At that moment a shadow fell on the page. Tom Sawyer stepped in the door and caught a glimpse of the picture. Becky snatched at the book to close it, and had the hard luck to tear the pictured page half down the middle. She thrust the volume into the desk, turned the key, and burst out crying with shame and vexation.

"Tom Sawyer, you are just as mean as you can be, to sneak up on a person and look at what they're looking at."

"How could *I* know you was looking at anything?"

"You ought to be ashamed of yourself, Tom Sawyer; you know you're going to tell on me, and oh, what shall I do, what shall I do! I'll be whipped, and I never was whipped in school."

Tom stood still, rather flustered by this onslaught. Presently he said to himself:

"What a curious kind of a fool a girl is! Never been licked in school! Shucks. What's a licking! That's just like a girl – they're so thin-skinned and chicken-hearted. Well, of course *I* ain't going to tell old Dobbins on this little fool, but what of it? Old Dobbins will ask who it was tore his book. Nobody'll answer. Then he'll do just the way he always does – ask first one and then t'other, and when he comes to the right girl he'll know it, without any telling. Girls' faces always tell on them. They ain't got any backbone. She'll get licked. Well, it's a kind of a tight place for Becky Thatcher, because there ain't any way out of it." Tom conned the thing a moment longer, and then added: "All right, though; she'd like to see me in just such a fix – let her sweat it out!"

After lunch a whole hour drifted by, the master sat nodding in his throne, the air was drowsy with the hum of study. By and by, Mr Dobbins straightened himself up, yawned, then unlocked his desk and reached for his book. He fingered it absently for a while, then took it out and settled himself in his chair to read. Tom shot a glance at Becky. He had seen a hunted and helpless rabbit look as she did, with a gun levelled at its head. Instantly he forgot his quarrel with her. Quick – something must be done! Done in a flash, too! But the very imminence of the emergency paralyzed his invention.

Too late. The next moment, the master faced the school. Every eye sunk under his gaze. There was that in it which smote even the innocent with fear. There was silence while one might count ten; the master was gathering his wrath. Then he spoke:

"Who tore this book?"

There was not a sound. One could have heard a pin drop. The stillness continued; the master searched face after face for signs of guilt.

"Benjamin Rogers, did you tear this book?"

A denial. Another pause.

"Joseph Harper, did you?"

Another denial. Tom's uneasiness grew more and more intense under the slow torture of these proceedings. The master scanned the ranks of boys – considered a while, then turned to the girls:

"Amy Lawrence?"

A shake of the head.

"Gracie Miller?"

Another negative. The next girl was Becky Thatcher. Tom was trembling from head to foot with excitement and a sense of the hopelessness of the situation.

"Rebecca Thatcher" [Tom glanced at her face – it was white with terror] – "did you tear – no, look me in the face" [her hands rose in appeal] – "did you tear this book?"

A thought shot like lightning through Tom's brain. He sprang to his feet and shouted,

"*I* done it!"

The school stared in perplexity at this incredible folly. Tom stood a moment, to gather his scattered faculties; and when he stepped forward to go to his punishment the surprise, the gratitude, the adoration that shone upon him out of poor Becky's eyes seemed pay enough for a hundred floggings. Inspired by the splendour of his own act, he took without an outcry the most merciless flaying that even Mr Dobbins had ever administered;

and also received with indifference the added cruelty of a command to remain two hours after school should be dismissed – for he knew who would wait for him outside till his captivity was done, and not count the tedious time as loss, either.

Tom fell asleep that night with Becky's latest words lingering dreamily in his ear –

"Tom, how *could* you be so noble!"

Adapted from The Adventures of Tom Sawyer, *the American classic by Mark Twain. Tom is an archetypal modern day hero!*

Exercise: Whose Story Is This?

When you write or tell a story, you will generally have a hero/ine... and a villain. Your main character will be the one whom you find most interesting: the one whom you want to talk about. Your protagonist is the person whose story you are telling. They may be a goodie or a baddie. What makes them important is that you relate the story from their point of view. You can only show what they see; you can only tell their thoughts and emotions. Other characters may report events that happened out of sight, or declare other ideas and feelings. These things are subsidiary information: you can only be sure of what the main character sees, feels and thinks.

Your protagonist can relate their story in the first person ('I'). Alternatively, you may choose to use the third person ('S/he'). In this case the protagonist is usually introduced right at the beginning, because the audience needs to know whose viewpoint they are getting. Short stories work best with a single protagonist. It is too confusing if you keep changing viewpoint all the time. In novels an author can shift viewpoint, so long as it is obvious who is speaking in each section. This can be used to give different perspectives on the same facts, as a way of raising tension. The protagonist of a story typically has an antagonist, who works against them. This opposition helps to make an interesting story. If the reader gets the antagonist's point of view, their perception of the main character may shift radically.

It is a good exercise to experiment with different viewpoints. If you are a writer, choose an episode from a piece you are working on. Take the viewpoint of a minor character who observes the scene. If you are a speaker or storyteller, take the villain from a favourite tale – Jack's Giant, for example. Take their perspective and tell the story from this new angle. Use the first person ('I') to really understand their point of view. Describe the action as you now see it. What actually happens? What do you think about it? How does that make you feel?

When you have finished, reflect for a few moments on what you have seen and heard.

Have you learnt an ything new about your subject? How can you use this in your work?

The Trickster

You make your own luck.

Perspectives

Three men walk into a bar and order a drink. The barkeeper puts a glass on the counter and brings out a bottle of his finest whisky. He fills the glass exactly to the half-way mark, and says,

"My friends, what do you make of this?"

The Scotsman says dourly,

"Och, it's half empty. I'll not be paying for that."

The Welshman says companiably,

"Cheer up, boyo. Glass half full, more like."

The Irishman picks up the glass, swirls it around, sniffs deeply and drains it in one draught.

"Fine stuff. I'll have some more of that," he says.

Carpe potum, seize the drink, as the saying goes.

Jungle Safaris

If you want to discover your inner self, get close to nature. Chitwan National Park in southern Nepal has rhinos, tigers and monkeys galore. If you're a rich tourist, you may see these from the comfort of an elephant's back or the safety of a jeep. The poor backpacker can take a jungle walking tour. Your local guide leads the way through scrubby grassland towards the banks of the Narayani River. On the way he briefs you about safety procedures. You start to hope the rhinos will stick to their jungle homes. After some time you come to the edge of the river. The muddy waters swirl vapidly past. Apparently crocodiles like to lurk just beneath the surface. When a deer comes to drink, they lunge out to seize it. They grow to monstrous size and can put on a surprising turn of speed. If a crocodile appears, the guide advises, find a tree to climb. You look around: there are no trees to be seen. The guide laughs: you will be amazed, he says, how fast you can find a tree.

The group of tourists had opted for a jeep tour. They had driven all morning and seen plenty of birds, some deer and what could have been a sloth bear in the distance. They had taken plenty of photos and drunk coffee from shiny thermos flasks. Now nature was making her predictable call. When the jeep next stopped, two men slipped out and walked a discrete distance into the trees. And there, finally, they saw the elusive tiger. The great beast was rather too close for comfort. The first man froze, hands in the air. The second dropped his daypack, kicked off his boots and turned to sprint.

"Are you mad?" hissed his companion. "You can't run faster than a tiger."

"I don't have to," came his reply. "I only have to run faster than you."

Apocryphal travellers' tales.

Tobacco for Sharing

Long ago, Gluka lived with his Grandmother in a small lodge on the edge of the water. Grandmother was old but she was very wise. One day she said to him,

"My grandson, it is a shame that we have no tobacco."

"What is tobacco, Grandmother?" he asked.

"Ah, tobacco is a gift from the Great Spirit who made us. Tobacco is a medicine plant. When you pray and burn tobacco, the smoke carries your thoughts up to heaven. When you smoke tobacco with friends, it induces a feeling of peace. When old people smoke tobacco, they see all the happy days of their lives in the pictures that curl up from the pipe. Tobacco is a very great blessing when it is used as the Maker intended."

"Then we shall have tobacco," said Gluka. "Where can I find it, Grandmother?"

"Ah, tobacco is not easy to find. It grows on an island out in the big water. It is guarded by an evil sorcerer who keeps it all for himself."

"Then I will make him share it," said Gluka.

He went and made a canoe, and pushed it out onto the water. Then he climbed into the canoe, and it shot over the waves towards the island. As he travelled across the water, Gluka sang:

"Sorcerer, you are going to travel.

"Sorcerer, you must leave your home.

"Sorcerer, you are going to travel.

"Sorcerer, you have gone away."

He sang this song four times, and when he finished it had come true. Gluka landed on the island and the sorcerer was not there. The cooking fire was out and a beautiful clay pipe decorated with bright colours lay beside it on the ground. Gluka picked up the pipe and put it in his pouch. He took the tobacco bundles which were drying on racks and stored them in his bag. He pulled up the plants in the tobacco fields around the lodge and stacked them in his canoe. Then he climbed back into the boat and it flew back across the waves towards his home.

"See, Grandmother," he said, "I have brought tobacco for the people."

Grandmother was very happy. But as she praised her grandson, the sorcerer appeared in a magical flying canoe. He was shouting in a terrible voice:

"WHERE IS THE THIEF WHO HAS STOLEN MY TOBACCO?"

Gluka was not frightened. He reached up and seized the edge of the canoe, and grasped the sorcerer in a bear hug.

"Welcome," he said. "You have given your tobacco for us to share. Now all the people will have tobacco to enjoy." And he squeezed so hard that the sorcerer shrank to the size of a grasshopper. Now he could only speak in a small squeaky voice.

"Please give me some seeds so that I can still grow some for myself."

Gluka shook his head.

"Now my children and my children's children will grow tobacco. But since you were the first to grow it, I will give you enough to enjoy in your lifetime. Open your mouth and receive your share."

So Gluka filled Grasshopper's mouth with tobacco, and split his coat so that he had wings to fly across the sky. To this day people grow tobacco, and when they use it just as the Maker intended, it is a good plant. As for Grasshopper, he flies around on the wings Gluka made him and chews his mouthful of tobacco. And if you ever pick up a grasshopper it quickly spits out some tobacco juice to say,

"See, I remember to share!"

A Native American story from the Abenaki who lived around Vermont and New Hampshire. The Trickster is here portrayed as a culture hero: although his actions seem destructive, they ultimately benefit mankind.

Fox and Crow

One day, Fox was out walking when he saw Crow sitting in a tall tree. Crow had a large piece of cheese in his mouth, and Fox felt very hungry. He sat down under the tree and looked up admiringly.

"Crow, dear fellow," he called. "How well you look today. The sun is shining on your wings. Your eyes are bright as two black beetles."

Crow was flattered. He puffed his feathers and rocked

sideways on the branch.

Fox continued: "If only I could hear you sing! I'm sure your voice would be as fine as the rest of you. What do you say, my friend?"

Crow opened his mouth to reply. The cheese tumbled to the ground. Fox seized it and ran.

Now Crow felt hungry...

A Belgian fable. 'Caveat emptor' (buyer beware) means you get what you want – but it may not be the best way to create customer loyalty...

Tar Dolly

Brer Rabbit liked nothing better than a fresh juicy turnip. Farmer Fox had planted a field full of them, and each morning Brer Rabbit would help himself to several as he passed by. Now, Farmer Fox would not have minded missing one or two – in fact, he might not even have noticed. But this constant pilfering was starting to annoy him and he determined to catch the culprit.

He took a great lump of sticky black tar and shaped it into a round fat dolly. It had chubby cheeks and plump arms and a soft squashy bottom. He put it in the grass on the edge of the field and it sat there looking very happy.

Next morning when Brer Rabbit came past he saw the tar dolly smiling at him. Inquisitive as ever, he went over to have a closer look.

"Hello there," he said. "You're a cute little thing." And he pinched its cheek.

The tar dolly sat there grinning but it didn't say a word. Brer Rabbit's hand was stuck to its cheek and he began to feel annoyed.

"Won't you talk to me then?" he asked, and he buffed it on the shoulder. Of course his hand stuck there too, and now he was frustrated.

"Too good for me, are you?" he cried, and he kicked its bottom. The tar dolly still didn't speak but it held on to his foot, and by now Brer Rabbit was furious.

"Let me go!" he shrieked, and whacked it hard with his other foot. So then he was properly caught and there was nothing he could do but wait and berate that heartless tar dolly.

In a while Farmer Fox came along on his morning walk. How he laughed to see Brer Rabbit hugging tar dolly.

"Now I've got you!" he yelled. "What shall I do with you? What sauce goes best with roast rabbit?"

Now, Brer Rabbit could see he had been tricked. He was in a difficult position but he was never one to give up, and he was thinking hard.

"Oh, Farmer Fox," he called. "You've caught me, indeed you have. But please have mercy now. Whatever you do, don't throw me into the bramble patch. How those thorns would scratch me!"

"Ha ha!" laughed Farmer Fox. "That's just what you deserve! Thank you for suggesting it!"

And he picked up Brer Rabbit, with the tar dolly still sticking to him, and threw him into the heart of the brambles.

And there the tar dolly stuck fast on the thorns and Brer Rabbit was able to pull his paws free. Thanks to his thick fur, the thorns never hurt him in the least. The tar dolly smiled at the sky whilst Brer Rabbit slunk off into the undergrowth. After that, whenever he took a turnip he was careful not to leave the top lying around.

Brer Rabbit is an archetypal Trickster figure: greedy and cunning, he still appeals to us because he makes us laugh. In West Africa the trickster figure is Anansi, the spider. When African slaves came to work on the plantations of North America they discovered a Native Rabbit trickster figure: they told new stories about him and the most famous Trickster hero was born.

Bringing Back Fire

Back in the beginning, all the fire was kept by four Fire Beings who lived on a great mountaintop up in the sky. The people down below had no fire: that meant no cooked food, no torch light and no way of keeping warm. In winter they got very cold indeed and the children cried miserably.

Coyote was a rascal but he did have a heart inside that furry chest. He felt sorry for the wailing children and besides, they kept him awake at night. After much thought, he decided that people needed his assistance. So he called a council of all the animals and asked for some volunteers to help him fetch fire for mankind.

"I can run fast," said Deer.

"I can climb well," said Squirrel.

"I am very nimble," said Chipmunk.

"And I am cunning," said Coyote. "Between us, we have everything covered."

So the four animals set off through the woods towards the mountain where the Fire Beings lived. When they came to the edge of the forest, Coyote told Squirrel to wait at the foot of a pine tree. They crossed a rocky valley where Coyote told Chipmunk to hide by a great boulder. They travelled across a wide plain and at the far side, Coyote told Deer to stand at the bottom of the mountain.

Coyote climbed the steep path and crossed the scrubby land at the top of the mountain. Just where it touched the sky, he saw the four Fire Beings sitting around their fire. It was getting dark now, so he could see them clearly outlined against the flames. They had dug a hollow and surrounded the fire with stones so that none could escape, except for the sparks which flew up into the air and made stars in the night sky. Coyote crept forward carefully until he was right behind the nearest Fire Being, and then he coughed loudly. All four of them leapt in the air and whilst they were getting over their surprise, Coyote spoke.

"Oh Glorious Ones," he crooned, "How splendid your camp looks! May I warm my poor cold paws beside you?"

The Fire Beings were flattered, and before they had time to think it through, Coyote was sitting next to them beside the fire. He edged forward until his feet were almost touching the flames. He pretended to be lulled by the warmth, and curled up with his head on his paws. His nose got so hot that he curled his tail around to protect it. It burned in the heat, and to this day Coyote has a black tip to his tail. The Fire Beings soon got used to him lying there, and they carried on talking about their own concerns. When he was sure they were not paying him any attention, Coyote opened one eye and saw a great big branch just inches away from his muzzle. Suddenly he jumped up, seized the end of the branch between his teeth and fled across the mountain. The Fire Beings leapt to their feet and ran after him, shouting terrible curses. Coyote tumbled down the path and came to the place where Deer was waiting. His legs were trembling and his lungs were raw but he managed to hold up the flaming brand.

"Pass it on!" he panted, and sank onto the ground.

The four Fire Beings passed him without a glance, chasing after Deer. They sped over the grass like a blaze with the wind behind it. Deer ran so fast that the flames streamed out behind him like a comet. They singed his tail, and to this day, deer only have short stubby little tails. He raced across the plain but the Fire Beings were gaining on him. When he reached the rocky valley, Chipmunk jumped out from behind his boulder. By now the branch had burnt down to a single twig, and Deer was coughing from the smoke.

"Pass it on!" he gasped.

Chipmunk took the twig between his teeth and skipped off over the stones. The Fire Beings were so close that one of them reached out and clawed Chipmunk's back: you can still see the dark stripes on his fur. Chipmunk dodged away and they lost sight of him among the rocks. That held them up for a few moments while he got to the edge of the forest. Squirrel was waiting at the foot of his pine tree, but by now the twig had burnt down to a single red-hot stick.

"Pass it on," choked Chipmunk, dropping the burning stick on the ground.

Squirrel seized the glowing embers in his mouth and scampered up the trunk. He got so hot that his tail curled right up over his back, and that's how squirrels still look today. Squirrel could see the Fire Beings stamping around below, and he knew that he had to hide the fire fast. Right at the top of the tree was a little hole and he spat the last sparks into it.

"Pahhh... Pass it on," he whispered, patting the fire-seeds into the soft wood. Then the fire was safely hidden, and all the animals stayed very quiet. Eventually the Fire Beings gave up their search and went back to the top of the mountain. Coyote taught people how to get fire out of the tree again by twisting two sticks to make a spark, and how to feed the flame with twigs to make a blaze. He hid fire-seeds in other trees too, so that people would always be able to make a camp-fire. Now mankind had hot food, and bright torches, and the children were warm on winter nights. Coyote is a terrible trickster, but we must always be thankful to him for the gift of fire.

A Native American story with many local variations. Here, Trickster is again a culture hero whose deeds benefit mankind.

Thor's Lost Hammer

One day Thor's hammer was missing.

"Theft!" thundered Thor. "Who dares to steal Mjollnir?"

"I shall find it," vowed Loki, the trickster.

The gods of Asgard were agitated. Thor's hammer Mjollnir was his greatest weapon in their battles with the Ice Giants.

Forged by the dwarves, it always hit its mark; guided by magic, it always flew back to his hand.

Loki set forth and came at last to the palace of Thrym, King of the Ice Giants. When Thrym heard Loki's mission, he smiled complacently.

"Yes, I have Thor's hammer. It is buried deep beneath my throne. You may have it back when the gods send Freya the Beautiful to be my bride."

Loki returned to Asgard, where the gods waited to hear his tidings.

"I have good news," he told them. "Thrym has the hammer, but he will return it if Freya consents to marry him."

"Wonderful!" roared Thor. "Freya, make ready for your wedding!"

Freya, tall and lovely, looked Thor straight in the eye.

"Go to hell," she said.

Thor flushed with rage, but Loki held him by the arm.

"The Giant King demands a bride. We must send one to him." Loki paused for a moment in thought. "Freya is tall; she is fair; none other will satisfy him. But as befits a virgin, her beauty must be hidden by a veil." The other gods sniggered, and he went on. "Her appetites are great: she will doubtless enjoy the wedding feast. When she has eaten and drunk, her companions will demand the bride price. Thrym will lay the hammer in her lap. When Freya removes her veil, the Ice Giants will learn the true cost of their demands."

"What do you mean?" cried Freya. "I will never marry an Ice Giant!"

"Indeed," said crafty Loki. "For it is Thor who will be sitting in the bridal seat."

There was a moment's silence, and then the gods burst out laughing.

"Freya," demanded Thor, "Lend me your largest gown..."

Loki the Trickster is a central figure of Viking mythology. Clever and devious, he was a half-blood himself but his cunning schemes often saved the gods. This story goes on to relate how Loki accompanies Thor to the Ice King's palace, dressed as his bridesmaid. The false bride wreaks a terrible vengeance on the Giants for their presumption, just as Loki had planned. You might like to carry on with this story, using the props technique in the exercise below.

Exercise: Talk It Through

Trickster, joker, charlatan... the fool has many faces. In his medley coat of many colours, the jester is the only man who can tell truth to the king. Wearing his carnival mask, he can do as he likes without fear of recrimination. Some of his manifestations are helpful or amusing; others have a more malevolent aspect. This ambivalent nature is part of the Trickster's appeal, but it also makes him a dangerous figure.

In many stories and books, the villain is a Trickster figure. Wild and anarchic, he is an intriguing counterpart to the clean-cut hero. His presence provides a piquant dash of danger. Although he is hard and selfish, you can identify with his choices. He behaves as you might like to if you were not afraid of the consequences.

When you are drawing a villain, it is important to understand him. This is true of all your characters, but it can be harder to consciously identify with someone you don't approve of. One way of working with diverse characters is to develop them through their possessions.

You know that cardinal rule 'Show, not tell'? You can use it to inspire yourself too! In this exercise, you are going to generate speech using props to personify the people involved. Remember that dialogue is a key skill for writers; a great tool for speakers and storytellers.

For this exercise, identify two characters who are going to come into conflict. They can be people from your story, or random figures who you want to develop. Try to choose individuals who will have quite different views of the world. Choose a prop to represent each character: a broad sunhat, a colourful cravat, some sequinned sandals… charity shops are a great source of material.

Next, set the scene: what are your characters going to argue about? Make it something suitably dramatic: your villain needs to have behaved badly. Maybe they smashed into the other's car; or were seen taking something from their bag; or claimed credit for their efforts at work.

Place two chairs opposite each other, and put one prop on each chair. The argument is about to start: now you're really going to get into character. Put on one person's item of clothing and sit in their chair. Become that character for the moment. How does it feel to be that person? How do you sit, what can you see, what are you thinking? Start talking to the 'person' opposite you. When you've had your say, it's their turn. If you can work with someone else, stay in character for the whole exercise. If you are working alone, use the props to shift between positions. Move to the other chair and put on that item: how do you feel now? Enter fully into this new point of view. Answer your accuser: you may be surprised at your response. After the argument is finished, come back into the role of narrator and think about what you have learned.

This process emphasizes the importance of understanding the characters in your story.

The Wise One

The tongue is mightier than the fist.

Aches and Pains

Fred and Bill were old friends. Every Sunday they met for a drink. They always sat in the same corner, sharing their foes and woes.

That night, Bill was feeling his age even more than usual.

"My back's killing me," he complained. "And my feet are sore. My arms ache from pushing that lawnmower, and I've got a blister on my thumb from those garden shears."

"Ah well," said Fred companionably. "Make the most of it. Soon we won't be feeling anything at all."

It never hurts to be reminded!

Perfect World

One of Gandhi's entourage was always fussing about this or that. Finally, the great man called him aside.

"I appreciate your concern," he said. "But perhaps we should try to be more flexible. Which is easier, to carpet the entire earth or to put on a pair of slippers?"

One day Gandhi was waiting on a railway platform with a large number of followers. The train finally arrived, but in the crush one of his shoes was knocked off. It fell down into the gap between the track and the platform. Gandhi calmly kicked his other shoe after it and stepped aboard.

"Why on earth did you do that?" one of his retinue asked. "You've lost a good pair of shoes."

"We could not wait for the next train," Gandhi replied. "And what use is a single shoe to a poor man?"

Anecdotal stories. Quietly insightful, Gandhi embodies the figure of the Wise Man for many people.

The Old Bedouin

Biggles landed his biplane neatly on the desert sands. He climbed out, took off his goggles and unfastened his flying jacket. The sun glared down like a resentful deity. Biggles sauntered over to the palm trees beside the oasis. An old Bedouin man sat in the shade watching him.

"Hello," said Biggles. "Do you speak English?"

"A little," the man replied.

"Good! I'm hungry. Have you any food?"

The Bedouin rose slowly and went to his bags. He unpacked dates, bread, some hard cheese. The meal was simple and conversation limited. Nevertheless, Biggles felt replete and profoundly satisfied.

As he stood to go, he asked,

"So where are you heading?"

"Cairo," the man replied.

"Me too! How long will it take your camel train to get there?"

"Within one week, Allah willing," came the answer.

"Ha! In my flying machine, I will be there this afternoon," boasted Biggles.

"Indeed?" the old man replied politely. "And what will you do with the time you save?"

Apocryphal tale that leaves your audience thinking.

The Natural Order

There once lived a great and powerful king. He had everything his heart could desire – rich lands, priceless jewels, beautiful wives – but still he was not content. One day he heard of a wise sage who lived in the mountains and resolved to ask his advice. He set out with a cohort of trusted soldiers and journeyed to the cave where this man lived. The old man hobbled out and regarded his visitors calmly. His back was so bent it was hard to tell whether he actually bowed as protocol demanded. The regent fixed him with an imperious stare.

"I have come to ask you a very important question," the king declared. "Tell me: What is the purpose of life?"

The sage thought for a moment. Then he picked up a stick and wrote in the sand.

Father dies.

Son dies.

The king was perplexed, and feeling foolish made him angry.

"Do you know who I am?" he shouted. "Is this all you have to say?"

The wise man stooped again, swept away the first line and wrote something else.

The words in the sand now read in reverse.

Son dies.

Father dies.

"Would you prefer it this way around?" he inquired.

Buddhist teaching tale.

Weather Vane

Down Under, it was April and the tribe were preparing for the winter months. The Aboriginal elders weren't expecting a hard winter, but they weren't up with modern weather forecasting technology. One chief's son was just back from college, so to be on the safe side they asked his opinion. Now, the young man didn't want to look foolish so he made a long-distance call to the Bureau of Meteorology.

"G'day," he said. "Can you tell me what the winter is going to be like this year?"

"Well," replied the weatherman, "We're predicting a few frosty days."

So the young man told the elders that there was going to be some cold weather. The elders told the people to expect a cold snap, and advised them to gather firewood. A couple of weeks later, just to be sure, the young man rang the Bureau of Meteorology again.

"G'day," he said. "What's winter going to be like? What are your satellites saying?"

"It's going to be cold," answered the weatherman. "We're predicting some really bad weather."

So the young man tipped off the elders, and they told the people to collect as much firewood as they could.

Another couple of weeks passed, and the cold spell still hadn't started. Just to be certain, the young man rang the Bureau again.

"G'day," he said. "What's this winter looking like? Is the cold weather coming soon?"

"We don't know when," the weatherman admitted. "But it's definitely going to be one of the coldest winters ever."

"How can you tell?" the young man asked.

"It's like this," the weatherman replied. "Our satellite pictures show that the Aborigines up north are gathering firewood like billy-oh. They always know what's coming."

Prophecies can be self-fulfilling, as in this apocryphal Australian anecdote.

The Old Fisherman

A millionaire is on holiday in Mexico. He hires a boat for a fishing trip. It's a great day out, and they catch plenty of fish. The group ends up having beers on the beach. The millionaire says to the fisherman,

"This is a great outfit you have here. You could really make something of it."

"What do you mean?" says the fisherman.

"Well, if I was you, I'd take a loan and get a bigger boat. With the revenue from that, you could buy more boats – a whole fleet. Start doing some serious fishing. Expand the scale of your operation, y'know what I mean? Maybe set up a fish-canning factory. Get into the export business. Make a lot of money. Then you could live the good life. Go on holiday to exotic places. Sit on the beach having beers with your friends. Relax!"

"Sounds good," says the fisherman, nodding.

"But I'll stay as I am..."

Here the basic five-point technique has been expanded, but the same structure applies. See 'The Seamstress' (The Grandam) for a more elaborate version of this story.

Hiawatha the Unifier

When the first people came to the land of America, they did not know anything. They were hungry and frightened, and the Great Maker took pity on them. Taking human form, he descended to earth and spoke to the people.

"My children, you will flourish in this new land. You will be numerous as the leaves of a forest in summertime. You must now spread out and become great nations."

Taking a little girl by the hand, he walked towards the sun and all the people followed him. After some time he stopped by the banks of a river and told some families to build a longhouse there. These people became the Mohawk tribe. The Maker gave them corn, beans, squash and tobacco. He showed them how to plant, reap and pound corn into meal. He gave them dogs and taught them how to hunt. When he had fully instructed them in the necessities of life, he led the rest of the people onwards.

After another long journey they stopped in a valley surrounded by forests, and he told another group to build their village here. These people became the Oneida nation, and once more he gave them what was necessary for life. A third group he left by a big mountain, and they became the Onondaga people. A fourth party he left beside a great lake, and they formed the Cayuga tribe. And the final handful of families settled beside a beautiful river and grew into the mighty Seneca nation.

To each nation the Maker gave a special gift. To the Seneca he gave such swift feet that their hunters could outrun deer. To the Cayuga he gave canoes and the skill to guide them through turbulent water. To the Onondaga he gave strength, strategy and knowledge of the eternal laws. To the Oneida he gave craftsmanship in making weapons and weaving baskets, whilst to the Mohawks he gave expertise in shooting and hunting.

For many years the people lived happily, each performing his own skill. The Maker chose to live amongst them as a man, and he took the name of Hiawatha. He went from tribe to tribe counselling the people on how to live in balance with nature. But the eternal laws dictate that day alternates with night, life with death, harmony with disharmony. From the north, beyond the Great Lakes, came wild men who did not know how to plant crops or fire clay. Their way was to prey upon the fruits of those who laboured. They sprang upon the people like animals, and the tribes turned to Hiawatha for advice.

The five nations assembled on the shores of a great lake and lit the council fire. At last Hiawatha appeared, gliding across the waters in a birchbark canoe. On the prow stood a great white bird and as he landed it flew up into the sky, dropping feathers as it went. When the elders and wise men had seated themselves around the fire, Hiawatha stood in the middle of the circle and spoke.

"In the beginning, you were young and knew nothing. You settled apart and grew as many nations. You have learned much and become strong. But no tribe alone can withstand all enemies. Now you must unite again to face a common danger.

Remember that you are brothers. You must act together as one people.

Onondagas, you are a tribe of mighty warriors. Your strength is like that of a great pine tree, with deep roots and wide branches. You shall be the protectors and the first nation.

Oneida, your men are famous for their wisdom. They will give counsel to the tribes. You shall be the second nation.

Seneca, you are swift of foot and eloquent of speech. You are the spokesmen and the orators. You shall be the third nation.

Cayuga, you are cunning and skilled in managing canoes. Be the guardians of our rivers. You shall be the fourth nation.

Mohawk, you are foremost in planting beans and corn. You shall be the nourishers and the fifth nation.

Together, you must be like the five fingers of a warrior's hand joined in gripping a war club. Unite as one, and none will overcome you. Choose the wisest women of your tribes to be your clan mothers and peacemakers."

He stooped and picked up the white feathers which the great bird had dropped.

"By these feathers," he said, "You shall be known as the Kanonsionni, the People of the Longhouse."

Thus was the mighty League of the Five Nations born, and its tribes ruled over all the lands between the great river of the west and the eastern sea. Hiawatha left this earth soon afterwards but his teachings of peace and brotherhood survive in the hearts of his people.

A Native American tale. Haio Hwa Tha ('He Who Makes Rivers') was a sixteenth-century Mohawk chief and shaman. In 1715 the Tuscarora joined the League which became known as the Haudenosaunee. Their enemies called them Iroquois ('real snakes') because they were such feared warriors.

Good St Nick

It had been a good night. The wine was sweet and the barmaids obliging. Nick staggered slightly as he stepped into the street. A full moon hung low above the rooftops. The cool air was welcomely refreshing. Nick waved away the servant who stood waiting and set off alone through the quiet streets.

His way passed through a poorer part of town. He stumbled on the rough ground and bumped against a wall. As he steadied himself, he heard a girl's voice from the window high above.

"That's all I really want."

Without thinking, Nick paused to listen. What women really want: that would be good for a young man to know!

Another girl answered, speaking low.

"Three gold coins! Father will never find so much for each of us."

"Without a dowry, his family will never let him marry me."

A third voice chimed in.

"There's only one way for girls like us to make money."

"And he would never want me after that..." The girl's voice dissolved in tears.

Nick bowed his head in confusion. Three gold coins: why, he had three times that in his purse at the end of a night out. To these sisters, it was the difference between life and despair. He pulled the little bag of money from his belt. Should he call up to them, throw it through the window? But they might be scared, ashamed at having been overheard. Better to leave it secretly, where they would find it in the morning. How to show their father that this was for his girls to share? Nick stood on one foot: wobbling, he pulled off one silk slipper, then the other. Swiftly he filled them with coins, twisted each into a ball, and threw the three little sacks over the courtyard wall. He heard them land with soft tinkling sounds. Then he ran down the street, his bare feet thudding on the ground, laughing like a schoolboy.

From that night onwards, Nick was a changed man. He still liked the good life: he could drink and sing with the best of them. But he seemed gentler, more interested in other people. When he heard a story of hardship, there was often another tale next night of unexpected generosity, an unseen benefactor who had helped in hidden ways. No-one knew who gave these gifts: they were always left in secret, without the expectation of thanks.

Nicholas joined the Christian Church and rose to become Bishop of Myra, in south-west Turkey. He was eventually canonized, although his full title sounds a little formal: the children whom he loved shorten Santa Nikolas to Santa Claus. The three bags of gold are echoed in the three gold balls found outside a pawnbroker's shop, giving people another chance in life. To this day, millions of people around the world help Nicholas in his work. At Christmas time they give gifts to children just to make them smile. Forget about magical flying reindeer: now that's a real miracle.

As You Find It

At the top of the hill, the traveller paused. Down before him spread the houses of a small town. A wrinkled peasant leant on the fence nearby, watching him.

"What's this place like?" the newcomer asked abruptly.

"What was the last place like?" the old man inquired.

"Terrible," he replied. "Full of liars, thieves and cheats. I couldn't wait to get out."

The old man regarded him ruminatively.

"I think you'll find this place much the same," he said.

The traveller frowned and went on his way.

Next day another traveller passed along the same road. He also paused by the old man, looking at the roofs below.

"What's this place like?" he asked.

"What was the last place like?"

"A great town. Met some nice people, had a good time. I was sorry to leave."

The old man chewed thoughtfully on his straw.

"I think you'll find this place much the same."

Wherever you go, you take yourself with you.

Exercise: Few Words

Wisdom can mean knowing what matters. This is a short task, and a very enjoyable one.

You are going to compose a poem. Not a long, narrative poem with a strict metric form. Nor a string of forced rhyming couplets. This is going to be a classical Japanese poem, a haiku.

The form of the haiku is very simple. It must have precisely seventeen syllables, spread over three lines (5, 7, 5). Traditionally the haiku is written about some striking sight or object, encapsulating the transient experience.

Select your object of inspiration. A flower is a good place to start. Jot down several adjectives which describe it for you. See if any of them inspire metaphors in your mind's eye. Select three of these aspects, and play with fitting them into the haiku form. If it doesn't fall into place, simply start again. Haiku are a high art form, but they are also great fun. Here is an example:

Haiku on Haiku

Short and beautiful.
That is all you need to know –
Capture the moment.

The Ogre

Be good, or the bogeyman will get you.

Burning the Books

The First Emperor of China did many things. He introduced a common currency, and standardized weights and measures across his realm. He built the Great Wall to keep out invading barbarian hordes. He also ordered that all books in his kingdom be burnt. In this way, people could not learn of other times and places which might compare more favourably with his own.

We must study history so that we do not repeat the same mistakes.

Over and Out

A US Navy gunboat was engaged in exercises off the coast of Canada when the following exchange of radio messages took place.

Operator #1: Calling unidentified craft. Recommend you divert your course 15 degrees north to avoid danger of collision.

Operator #2: Hello! Advise you divert your course 15 degrees south to avert collision.

Operator #1: Repeat message: Request you divert north now to avoid collision.

Operator #2: Repeat response: Suggest you divert south now to avoid collision.

Operator #1: This is the USS Enterprise. We are an aircraft carrier of the US Navy. Instruct you to divert north NOW!

Operator #2: We are a Canadian lighthouse. Over to you!

This story may not appear to follow the 'five finger technique': in fact, the initial status quo and final denouement are left to the listener's imagination, with great comic effect.

The Rats of Hamlyn

In olden days, Hamlyn was a prosperous town. Merchants did good business in the main square. The river carried cargo boats and the road brought trade. The farmland around was rich and fertile. There was no cause to think these times would ever end.

But where there is surplus, there will be scavengers. One year, the harvest was especially generous. When the barns were filled to bursting, the rats came. Large black rats with scabrous tails and sharp yellow teeth. Nothing was safe from the vermin. They ate all the wheat in the grain stores. They gnawed through the bins in the kitchens. They chewed clothes and blankets in storage chests. They even bit the babies as they slept in their cribs.

The townsfolk were in despair. The mayor called a meeting of his council. All agreed that they must get rid of this pestilence. Every household would offer a gold coin as reward. Runners were sent far and wide to appeal for help.

Seven days later, a man appeared on the steps of the town hall. He was a strange figure: dark and thin, with patched clothes of many colours and narrow slanting eyes. Slung over one shoulder he carried a small sack. When the mayor asked his business, he replied that he had come to claim the promised prize.

"First you must earn it," the mayor announced. "Can you rid us of these rats?"

The man reached into his bag and drew out a flute. He put it to his lips and blew a long, low note. Then he walked down the steps and along the street, playing as he went. The rats came out of the houses and followed him. He passed through the town gate and walked down to the river. Stepping in, he stood amongst the swirling waters. The rats followed him and were all carried away by the current.

The man came back to the steps of the town hall. By now the townsfolk had gathered, drawn by the strange music. They stared at the slight figure in his patchwork cloak.

"What happens? Are the rats gone? That wasn't so difficult after all."

"No, indeed. He did little. Hardly worth the payment we proposed."

"Shady character. He'll probably take whatever he can get."

The mayor stepped forward uncertainly. There didn't seem to be any money forthcoming, and he could hardly subsidize the expense himself.

"Thank you, my good man. We will reward your services. One silver talent... Is that satisfactory?"

The stranger did not reply, but his lips curled in a half-smile. He held out his hand and stood waiting silently. The mayor pressed a silver coin into the outstretched palm. The man slipped it into his sack. Then he raised his flute to his lips once more and began to play.

This time the tune was a lilting melody. As the first notes tumbled from his pipe, the children ran to listen. They danced down the street behind the stranger as he strolled out of town. Their mothers watched indulgently, waiting for them to tire. The stranger passed through the town gate and turned beside the river. He led the children along the bank, playing as he went. The townsfolk waited in vain for their children to return that night. Not one of those who followed the piebald piper was ever seen again.

Hamlyn, a town in north Germany, still commemorates the loss of its children. They were probably lured away in the thirteenth century on the disastrous Children's Crusade to rescue the Holy Land from the infidels.

They Walk Among Us

The young angel was keen to learn more of mankind. He badgered his mentor until one day the older angel agreed that they should visit earth. On their first evening, the pair walked until the light had nearly faded. They came at length to a remote cottage in the hills. The old couple who lived there were poor, but they were glad to have company. They shared their meal of bread and cheese, washed down with water from the well. After supper, the visitors were ushered to the only bedroom where they slept comfortably on a pallet of fresh straw. However, they woke the following day to find their hosts lamenting bitterly. Their only cow had died in the night, and things would be hard for them. The angels bid them a subdued farewell, and went on their way.

The next evening, they came to a large house surrounded by rich gardens. The owners of the house were already at supper, and none too pleased at being disturbed. They told the cook to feed the travellers scraps from the table, and grudgingly gave them a place to sleep in the cellar. The next morning, the younger angel awoke to find his companion mending a hole in the cellar wall. He thanked their hosts profusely for their hospitality before they left. As they walked along, the younger angel could not contain his anger.

"Is this how we treat mankind?" he demanded. "That peasant couple, they gave us what they could, and yet we let them suffer. The rich family spared us nothing of any value, yet you repair their property. What sort of hypocrisy is this? Do we only allow sycophants to prosper? How can you reconcile this with the values we profess to represent?"

"My friend, do not be so hasty," replied his mentor. "Things are not always as they seem. You recall the old couple with whom we stayed? Death came that night for the wife: I persuaded him to take their cow instead. As for the rich man's house, that wall was crumbling because the last owner hid a treasure there. It will stay hidden a little longer now. You must learn to look beyond the appearance of things."

A Lot to Ask

Alcestis thought the world of her husband. Admetus was a brash type who was friendly with the sun-god Apollo. It was Apollo's idea to woo girls in a chariot drawn by a lion and a bear: cute cuddly creatures that Alcestis adored. It was Apollo who, when he heard Admetus was dying, persuaded the Fates to spare him if someone could be found to take his place.

Admetus asked his parents first: they were elderly and surely had little to live for. The old folk refused with some vehemence: hadn't they given him enough already? Shouldn't they be allowed to enjoy the time they had left? No-one else was willing to volunteer either, though Admetus promised quite a large reward. Alcestis felt she should at least offer, although obviously he would refuse. But he didn't: he accepted with surprising alacrity. She couldn't help wondering whether her husband loved her as much as she did him.

So poor pretty Alcestis lay down on her bed, and stopped breathing. The burial ceremony was held that afternoon: there wasn't much point hanging around in the summer heat. Admetus had to leave early, as he had an unexpected guest: his old comrade Herakles was passing by on one of his Labours, and had dropped in for supper.

Herakles was unaware that he had appeared at a sensitive time. He enjoyed a long hot bath and put on a clean toga. The banquet spread was superb, food prepared for the funeral feast.

The two friends had a lot to talk about. They were occasionally interrupted by wailing sounds, but Admetus dismissed them – "Mourners, yes: a foreign woman, no blood relative." His duty of hospitality came above all other obligations.

It was not until Herakles was preparing for bed that an old servant told him the truth. He was deeply moved by his friend's generous spirit and resolved to do what he could to help. Leaping up, he hurried along the path to the fresh tomb. A dark figure was bent over the shrouded body. Herakles called out: Death straightened up and looked around. He had not yet cut the thread which bound Alcestis to her soul.

"A challenge!" shouted Herakles, panting slightly from the climb. "Wrestle with me! If I beat you, give back the girl!"

Death slowly smiled. So often his job was dull and depressing: this was a novel development.

"The great Herakles! Yes, it would be interesting to see..."

He dropped his scythe and glided towards the hero. Herakles flexed his legs in a wider stance. Suddenly Death was upon him, gripping with bony hands, a vortex of icy darkness. Herakles fought desperately to throw his opponent, but it was all he could do to keep his own feet on the ground. For an hour they swayed, locked in a mortal embrace, more like lovers than lethal enemies.

At last Herakles felt the vice-lock slacken. He tried to grasp his rival, but the dark robes whirled through his hands like mist. Death stood apart, and though his face could not be seen, it seemed that he was smiling.

"A worthy opponent indeed," he purred. "Your reputation does you justice. I think we should call it a draw."

He nodded courteously, swung around and slipped off into the night.

Herakles stepped forward and picked up the girl's body. He could feel the spirit stir within her. It would be a while before she could speak: but it occurred to him that in the circumstances, Admetus might not object to having a dumb wife.

Who do you think was the ogre in this story?

An Appointment

A man was walking down the street when he saw Death coming the other way. The dark reaper stopped, consulted his list and finally shook his head.

"I'm not meeting you till tomorrow," he said.

Now, the man didn't want to die. He ran home, grabbed a bag and stuffed it full of clothes. He took a taxi to the airport and got on the next plane. He flew all night, across seas and over deserts, until he finally landed in Alexandria.

Feeling very pleased with himself, the man caught a bus into town. He found a hotel room, washed and shaved. Then he went out to get some breakfast.

Coming down the street towards him was a familiar figure in a black hood.

"Hello there," called Death. "I was surprised to see you yesterday! We've got an appointment here today..."

This is a traditional tale with many variations. It reminds us that sometimes we must accept things without wasting too much energy. In the words of St Francis of Assisi, "Lord, give me the courage to do what must be done; the patience to bear what cannot be changed; and the wisdom to know the difference."

The Good Host

Once there was an old farmer who lived all alone in the mountains. His wife had died and his children had long ago left home and gone to live in the city. He rose with the sun and often worked long after the stars were out. He had plenty to eat and friends in the village when he wanted company. All in all, it was a hard life but a good one.

One evening the old man was coming down from the pastures when he met Death on the path leading to his farm. Now, he loved this world but he knew better than to argue if his time was up.

"Hello," he stuttered, trying not to shake.

"Greetings," Death replied. "You're just the man I've been looking for."

"Well, so be it," said the farmer. "If you'll be kind enough to let me, there are a couple of chores I should finish." And hearing no objection, he led the way into the farmhouse.

Death sat down at the kitchen table and stretched his legs.

"Something smells good," he observed.

The farmer's hospitable heart was stirred.

"You must have travelled a long way," he cried. "Let me get you something to eat. Some pickles, maybe? A little bread and cheese? I have a stew on the stove if you would like some."

"That will do nicely," his visitor replied. So the old man went into his larder and filled a plate of his finest fare. He laid two places at the table, and uncorked a bottle of his best wine.

"I've been saving this for something special," he commented. "I can't think of a better occasion!"

Well, the supper was good and the room was warm. The two of them drank and talked far into the night. When at length the stars dimmed outside the window, the farmer drained his glass and stood up with a contented sigh. He turned off the stove, filled the dog's bowl and propped the door open. Death rose and adjusted his dark robes. He turned solemnly and stepped out of the farmhouse. The old man gave one last look around, squared his shoulders and set off behind him.

Half-way along the path, Death stopped and turned around.

"Why are you following me?" he inquired.

"Well, isn't that the protocol?" the farmer asked.

"Only when I summon you," Death replied.

"But I thought..." The old man stopped as Death gave a low

laugh.

"My thanks for a wonderful evening. Your hospitality merits some return. Luckily I had no other appointments last night. I'll be back one day, my friend. I look forwards to our next meeting."

And the Grim Reaper strode off down the valley.

Traditional eschatological story.

Exercise: Feel The Beat

Good stories have a rhythm that sweeps the action onwards. This is most obvious in narrative poetry. Literary epics such as Homer's *Iliad* and *Odyssey*, or the Saxon masterpiece *Beowulf*, propel the story forward with skilful use of metre and beat. The same principles apply in great prose, although the mechanism is harder to see. A good way to develop your instinctive sense of rhythm is to experiment with poetic forms.

Look at the opening lines of this classic poem by WH Auden:

"This is the night mail crossing the border,
Bringing the cheque and the postal order,
Letters for the rich, letters for the poor,
The shop at the corner and the girl next door,
Pulling up Beattock, a steady climb –
The gradient's against her but she's on time."

Read the poem aloud and see which syllables you naturally emphasize. Feel how the rhythm of the words evokes the sound of the train wheels; sense the engine strain on the hill – the sense of release when she makes it and the steady rhythm returns.

In this exercise you're going to write a few lines of poetry, focussing on the rhythm. Modern poetry doesn't have to rhyme, so you're free to play with the beat of the lines.

Your poem doesn't have to rhyme, but it must 'scan'. This means that you have to write it according to a metrical pattern. For this poem, use the rhythm of *The Night Mail* as a model. (You can make up poems with different beat patterns afterwards.) Start by writing down the first line:

"This is the night mail crossing the border..."

Who do you think is on the train?
What are they carrying?
Where is the train going?

Carry on writing until you have six or eight lines of poetry. Note how an even number of lines in this format gives a sense of wholeness or completeness.

Try reading your poem out loud. See whether it has the same rhythm that it did in your head.

Observe how certain words can change the emphasis of an entire line.

In a story, metre is most important in first and last lines. You can use it to set the tone at the start and to wrap up an incident. Metric couplets – two sentences with the same rhythm – provide initial impetus and present a final conclusion. See if you can devise a story ending with this pattern:

Di dah di dah di dah di dah
Di dah di dah di dah di dah

"And so the monster was destroyed. The town could rest in peace at last."

Think about how you could use rhythm, especially at the beginning and end of a story.

Stories For Sharing

May your mouth be full of stories, and your pocket full of stars.

Meats of the Ear

Once there lived two boys, and they were friends.

One was the son of a king, and lived in a big compound with armed guards surrounded by high walls; the other was the son of a poor peasant who lived just outside the compound; but every day when the young prince had finished his lessons and the poor boy had finished his work, they would play together until the sun set and they were both called home to have their suppers.

When they grew up the prince became king himself, and married the most beautiful girl in the land. She had a long slender neck and eyes like a doe. The king gave orders that she be dressed in bright robes of the finest fabric and adorned with the most wonderful golden jewelry that money could buy.

The poor boy married too: a good-natured girl from the village, not much to look at but always laughing. Although they had to work hard for a living, the couple were very happy together.

As the months and years passed, it could be seen that despite her life of luxury, the king's wife was slowly fading away. Her beautiful dark eyes grew dull, whilst she became thinner and thinner.

But the poor man's wife grew plumper and prettier, and was always smiling.

One day, the king rode out and asked his old friend what he did, that his wife was thriving so.

"Oh, that is simple," the poor man replied. "I feed her meats

173

of the ear."

Indeed, thought the king: that must be the best portion of meat, no fat and no muscle; I will also feed my wife only upon the choicest tid-bits. And he sent instructions accordingly to the palace kitchens.

But still the king's wife wasted away, and in the end, in desperation, the king commanded that his wife should be sent to live for a while with his old friend, to see whether life outside the palace should suit her any better. In exchange, he offered to let the plump good-natured peasant girl come to keep him company in the palace.

Indeed, at first the plan seemed to be working: for as the days and weeks passed, the king's wife grew visibly better. But as her health improved and her beauty returned, it could also be seen that the peasant girl was languishing in her place; for despite the good food in the palace her cheeks grew hollow, and though her life was now one of ease, she was never seen to smile.

For of course the 'meats of the ear' that the poor man fed his wife were words, stories that fed her heart and mind and soul even when her stomach was hungry.

When the poor man came home each day, he would greet his wife and talk with her, telling her of all he had seen that day; and he would recount funny anecdotes that made her laugh; and after supper he would sing songs and tell tales, to amuse her.

All day long, she would smile when she remembered the things that her husband had told her, and her cheeks were round with laughing and her skin shiny as a young girl's.

When these things were taken from her she fell into decline and grew ill, just as the king's wife had done before her.

For we cannot live without the stories that give meaning to our lives.

A traditional story from West Africa.

Schezerade

Once upon a time, there lived a king called Shahryar. His palace was splendid, and his lands were rich and prosperous. His brother ruled the neighbouring land of Samarkand, and each of them had a beautiful wife. The king thought that he was very happy.

One day Shahryar was seized by a violent longing to see his brother. He sent his vizier to Samarkand, asking him to visit. The brother was delighted to receive this invitation. He made due preparations and set out at once, with a string of camels bearing gifts. A few miles down the road, however, he realized that he had forgotten a particular treasure. Telling the caravan to continue without him, he rode swiftly back with only a few trusted men-at-arms. Arriving home, he ran straight up to his private quarters. Imagine his horror on entering the bedroom to perceive his wife in the arms of a huge slave. His eyes darkened and his heart turned to ice. Drawing his sword, he slew them both instantly. Then, without saying a word to anyone, he retrieved the treasure and rejoined his companions.

When he arrived, Shahryar greeted his guest with great affection. But his brother seemed distracted and could hardly reply. At first, the king thought that his guest was merely tired from his journey. But as the days passed, he began to suspect that there was some deeper reason. He arranged a hunting expedition, but his brother was too downhearted to accompany him. Left alone, he roamed around the palace disconsolately. Pausing at a window, he beheld the king's wife and her female attendants disporting themselves in the gardens below. Some swam in the sparkling fountains whilst others rested in the shade, feasting on fruits and ices. After a while, he beheld a crowd of male slaves approaching: each proceeded to embrace one of the women, with the largest man taking the king's wife.

The king's brother watched in amazement. After a while, he

said to himself:

"If this can happen to my brother too, then my misfortunes are not so unusual."

His spirits and his appetite were restored by this thought. He went downstairs and partook of a fine meal.

When Shahryar returned, he was pleased to find his brother in such a fine mood. He asked him whence this welcome reversal of spirits. At first his brother was loath to speak, but in the end he revealed the entire story. The king could hardly believe his ears, but a brother's word is trustworthy. The following day he arranged another hunting expedition, but this time he secretly concealed himself within the palace. Sure enough, he witnessed events just as his brother had related. With the evidence of this double betrayal, the king vowed that he would never trust a woman again. He ordered that the queen and all her attendants be put to death. From that day onwards, he ordered his vizier to bring him a virgin girl each evening to be his wife. Each morning afterwards, the girl would be put to death: that way he would never again suffer betrayal.

This went on for three years, until the kingdom had run out of suitable virgins. One day the vizier could not find a single girl to be the king's bride. He returned to his home in despair, for he feared the king's wrath. Now, the vizier had two daughters himself. The elder was called Schezerade, and she was both lovely and wise. In particular she loved stories: she had read many books, listened to countless poets and knew tales and songs from many lands. Schezerade was brave as well as beautiful, and she devised a plan.

"Father, you must take me to marry this king. Bring my little sister Dunzyad also. When the king has done with me, she will ask me for a story to pass the long hours of the night. Do not fear, for all will be well."

The vizier was filled with trepidation, but he really had no choice. All was made ready, and at nightfall he delivered the two girls to the king. Dunzyad sat quietly by the bedside until the king was satisfied. And when the time was right, she said:

"Dear sister, tell me one of your marvellous stories, so that the time may pass delightfully."

Then Schezerade began to tell a tale, and the king listened enraptured. But as dawn approached she yawned, and left the story at a point where the king longed to know what happened next. So he instructed that she was not to be killed until the following day. And in this way night followed night, each more entrancing than the one before. And each morning, the story stopped at a point where the king wanted to find out more.

Schezerade told stories of djinns and monsters, princes and peasants, good men and brave girls, villains and harlots. She told tales about tales, and stories within stories. She showed Shahryar the ways of the world and the vagaries of the human heart. For a thousand long warm evenings she wove a spell of words. And on the thousand and oneth night, she stopped.

Then Dunzyad slipped from the room and returned with a tiny boy, whilst behind her came a slave woman carrying twin infants in her arms. Schezerade set the babes down on the royal bed, saying,

"Dear lord, these are the sons whom Allah has sent us since I came to be your wife."

Tears ran down the king's face as he beheld their children. He took Schezerade in his arms and said,

"Dearest wife, you have cured my grief and won my heart. Live with me and be my queen. Your stories shall be written down and preserved for all posterity, for they are truly wondrous."

That day a royal decree was issued for a great feast in the city. All the people joined in the celebrations, both from joy for the royal couple and relief that the dreadful edict had been lifted. The king sent for his brother, who took Dunzyad as his bride.

The next night, Schezerade started another story...

A Thousand and One Arabian Nights *is a wonderful compilation of fantasies. It contains famous tales such as 'Sinbad the Sailor' and 'Ali Baba and the Forty Thieves', as well as a multitude of less well-known narratives. The earliest reference to this collection is in a Persian book dated 947 AD. Various other manuscripts are mentioned by different sources over the following centuries. The first printed version was a French translation by Antoine Galland in 1704 AD. Schezerade (or Schehezerade)'s stories are all magical, but her own – the frame story – is best of all.*

Stone Soup

It was a cold night. Stars stared down from a cloudless sky. The wind whisked around the scattered camp-fires, whispering to itself.

The girl took something from her bag and put it into her cooking-pot. Carefully she poured in water, and set the pot to simmer over the flames. Then she settled down to mend her shoe, worn bare on the long journey.

A few yards away, another girl watched enviously. She drew her robe tighter around herself, shivering. The first girl looked up and smiled.

"You look cold," she called. "Why don't you come and share my fire?"

They sat together, faces glowing in the warm light.

"You are kind. I have no food tonight. Times are hard."

"You are welcome to share my soup. Would you stir it for me?"

The newcomer rose and stirred the pot. She lifted a spoonful of steaming liquid to her lips, tasted it and added a pinch of salt from the pouch on her belt.

"You are fortunate to have food. The way is not easy."

The girl nodded. "I am fortunate indeed. I owe my luck to an old woman whom I met on the road here. I helped her to cross the river, and in return she gave me something very special."

"Do tell me more! What was it that she gave you?"

Close by, two children were trying to hear the story. They inched closer, until at last the firelight almost licked their toes. The girl laughed and beckoned them over. Their mother smiled gratefully. The Great Road could be hard, especially with small ones to care for. While they listened she stirred the pot and added a handful of dried herbs from her bag.

"I think she must have been a witch. She gave me something magic."

Another family appeared out of the darkness. The man spoke for them.

"Can we join you? The night is bitter and we have no firewood."

"Of course. Join us and share our food. There will be plenty for all."

"We have little to offer in exchange. Only a few vegetables for the pot."

"Whatever you have to give is welcome. Come and sit with us."

The group around the fire talked and laughed. Others joined them.

Some had food to contribute; others brought nothing but hungry eyes; yet all were made welcome and took turns to tell tales and tend the pot, adding whatever they could.

At last the girl rose, smelt the broth, tasted it and pronounced it ready. There was bread to share; every last drop and morsel was soon devoured.

"So what did the old woman give you?" they asked when it was all gone.

"She gave me a soup-stone so that I need never be hungry again."

And they all agreed that nothing had ever tasted better than stone soup.

This is an old folk-tale. Like the soup-stone, it is none the worse for repeated use.

Exercise: The Story Circle

You don't have to be a professional speaker or writer to share stories. Anyone can draw on their life experiences to tell a good tale. One of the best ways of getting people to share their stories is to make a 'storytelling circle'. This can be done in a training session or simply with a gathering of friends. Sit in a ring – around a table or in comfortable chairs – the setting doesn't really matter. Have something in the middle as a focal point: a candle works well, or fresh flowers. Make sure everyone is settled and happy to begin. Then turn to the first person and say,

"Tell me about…"

>   … a time when you were really happy.
>   … something that happened when you were very young.
>   … someone who deeply influenced you.
>   … how you met your current partner.
>   … why you decided to live in this town.
>   … a time when you were really angry.
>   … a time when you got completely lost.
>   … something you remember about your grandmother.
>   … your favourite game when you were a child.
>   … something good that happened to you last week.
>   … the most exciting thing you've ever done.
>   … the most difficult journey you ever took.
>   … a time you found something precious.
>   … a time when you were really scared.
>   … a time when you felt really down.
>   … the bravest thing you've ever done.
>   … the best holiday you've ever been on.

... a secret you've never told before.

... your first love.

This is a great ice-breaker if you're running a course, workshop or group event. Ask the participants to get into pairs and talk to each other. The material doesn't have to be shared publicly, but it's surprising how well people bond when they have exchanged stories.

These prompts also make great writing exercises. Set a timer and spend fifteen minutes on your chosen topic. If you are in a writing group, take it in turns afterwards to read aloud your work.

Part III: Practical Resources

Now it's time for you to tell a story. It can be any anecdote that you want to tell an audience. Perhaps you want to improve your presentation skills in the workplace. Maybe you need to make a formal speech at a social event. Perhaps you've been inspired to write a short story, or even a novel. If you have an experience or an idea that you want to relate, that's great. Use the tips and techniques in the first part of this book to get you going. If not, remember that professional speakers are always borrowing stories. The best tales in the world have already been told countless times: they just get better with each retelling. So start with your favourite fairytale, or choose a story from this book. You're going to change it, to make it your very own story.

Here goes...

Telling Your Story

This section is about telling stories to an audience. Perhaps you're giving a leadership presentation. Maybe you're running a training session. Or maybe you want to tell stories just for fun. Whatever the reason you're telling this tale, remember that stories work because they engage the imagination. Whether your story is meant to inspire, inform or educate, above all it must be entertaining.

A Story Session

So you've chosen a tale and decided on your audience. Now you're ready to tell your story. As a storyteller, you must present a show: 'un spectacle', as the French say. Make sure that you do your tale justice. Here are some of the things you need to remember.

Before you start, consider the setting for your story session. Are the time and place suitable for the tale you want to tell? Is everyone sitting comfortably? Do you have any props to hand? Think about what would be appropriate for your audience. In an informal setting, maybe use something as a prompt for your story: an ivory elephant, a pair of old binoculars. In a more formal setting, consider what you are wearing. Your clothes should be smart with an individual touch: this makes people more receptive to hearing a lateral viewpoint. Perhaps you want objects to illustrate your narrative: a hat to represent each character; a photograph to set the scene; a bell for sound effects. Have all these things ready to hand before you start telling your tale.

Your voice is your main instrument as a speaker. Always remember to 'talk loud, slow and low'. Speak loudly enough to be heard clearly by the whole group. In general, keep your voice 'slow and low': studies show that people respond more to a deeper voice (Margaret Thatcher had coaching to speak more effectively when she was Prime Minister). However, vary your tone to maintain interest. If you can mimic accents, use them for both impact and humour. Otherwise, change your pitch to show when different characters are speaking. The pace of your delivery should reflect the mood of the story. Silence builds suspense, and focusses attention. Pause at key points in the action, letting your audience relish the moment.

Involve your listeners by showing an interest in them. Make eye contact with the audience: look at individuals, speaking a few words to one person before moving your gaze to another. This shows that you care about keeping their attention. When you are talking directly to someone, it is very hard for them not to respond. Talking directly to someone also helps you adopt an expression appropriate to what you are saying.

Whilst you are telling the story, use gestures to link one thing with another. Paint a picture with your hands: Pointing into the distance, sweeping away imaginary barriers, holding up your palms in a rhetorical question ("What could he do?"). Your movements should be few, but intentional. Don't let your hands wander, as this can distract the audience. Ration your gestures to just those ones which further the action.

As you approach the end of your tale, wind up loose ends. How do you want your audience to remember the story? Was there a moral or a message? Plan your last line and deliver it in a clear voice. You may use a gesture of closure, such as putting your palms together, to indicate that the story is complete.

Stop talking and look around. Do not be tempted to say anything more at this point. After a few moments, move to a slightly different position. This indicates that you have entered a new stage of interaction, and the audience may start to talk.

Don't be self-conscious about storytelling. Your mouth is the medium, but the story encapsulates a truth which transcends your personal narration. This is particularly true of classic stories such as folk and fairy tales. When you tell a traditional tale, you will find that it has a momentum of its own. It is also true of archetypal stories like the ones in this book. You, the speaker, are weaving to a pre-existing pattern: you are simply a channel for the narrative.

Tips For Storytelling

Make the audience care what happens.

What do you know about your characters?

What does your audience need to know?

Use your Senses: How does it:
Look? Sound? Smell? Taste? Feel?

Adjectives vs. similes vs. metaphors.

Wherever possible, **SHOW NOT TELL**.

Everything you include should be relevant.

Rule of threes:
    Fractal patterns;
        try and try again;
            third time lucky.

'Story mountain' – build to climax.

After action, relieve the tension.

Every story needs a little humour.

Make notes! Don't rely on memory.

Put it away, wait a while, try it again.

Storytelling is painting with your voice.

Story Worksheet

A. Who is the story about?
Main character
      Name, appearance, personality
      Whose viewpoint? (1st or 3rd person)
Other significant characters
      (Archetypal figures)

B. Where and when will your version take place?

C. What happens in this story?
      What are the main events?
      How do they link together?
      Five Finger Technique

      Situation (Who, where, when)
      Something changes
      First...
            Next...
                  Finally...

      Resolution (outcome)
      Wrap-up: strapline.

D. How will you tell the story?
  Building rapport: relate to the audience
  What makes this story relevant to them?
  Striking images, similes, metaphors

E. Why are you telling this story?
  Is there a message or moral?
  How will your audience think / feel / act afterwards?

Whenever you start a story, these are the things you need to know. You might want to illustrate a point, convey a message or simply pass the time. If you tell stories often, you'll need to go through this planning process regularly. You can do it in moments using the 'five finger technique' as a story-planning mnemonic.

Creating Characters

If you want to tell vivid stories, you must have interesting characters. They need to be realistic: people that your audience can relate to. They will probably also be slightly simplified: larger-than-life figures who help to get your point across.

As the narrator, you should get to know your characters. You won't reveal all these details, but knowing them will make your stories much more realistic. The best way to bring your characters to life is to describe what they do. If you know that someone is mean, don't just say it: show them saying or doing something nasty. Remember that the most interesting plot twists often stem from a personal weakness. As the story progresses, your hero/ine will hopefully learn from their experiences. This means that they will change their behaviour: think about how you can show this personal development. It makes your character more believable – and hopefully your audience can learn from the story too.

One of the easiest ways to draw convincing characters is by using archetypal features. These provide a shorthand for your audience: they can easily recognize the wise mentor, the good mother, the hero and so on. This helps you to develop your story quickly and keep your listeners interested. There are many modern manifestations of the twelve archetypal figures. The main archetypal features, and contemporary manifestations of these figures, are listed below.

Archetypal Features

When you are developing your characters, keep in mind what archetypal roles they will play in your story. The main features of each figure, which make them easily recognizable to your audience, are outlined here. Some contemporary manifestations of these figures are listed over the page.

Princess – pretty but passive: she is defined by her demeanour, not by her crown.
Clever Girl – looks after herself: she has learnt how to make her own way in life.

Good Mother – caring for others: a fine balance between nurturing and suffocating.
Wild Woman – wants to have fun: enjoys life to the full, but may search for deeper meaning.

Grandam – gentle, kindly, venerable: a constant source of sympathy and support.
Wicked Witch – clever old crone: time has given her both wrinkles and knowledge.

Noble Youth – destined for greatness: behaves with natural grace and good manners.
Urchin – cheeky opportunist: survives by a combination of sharp wits and good luck.

Hero – honourable champion: brave and noble, he needs to keep his virility in check.
Trickster – wily and cunning: a joker and natural rebel, good often comes of his actions.

Wise One – sage and mentor: his age and experience means he can offer good advice.

Ogre – dark and malevolent: the shadow we project onto those who are different from us.

You can learn more about these archetypal figures, with examples of how they appear in well-known books, plays and films, in my book *LifeWorks*.

Contemporary Figures

These are some of the many modern manifestations which you may want to incorporate in your stories. They can have any face you please, although you will probably find that they emerge in keeping with 'type'. In anecdotes and short stories, characters are most effective in a single role. In books and plays, protagonists can have multiple dimensions. Sometimes they will even evolve from one archetypal figure to another. You can have fun subverting expectations and developing complex characters in your stories. The only limit is your imagination!

Princess – Pretty Maid; Perfectionist; Delicate Child; Spoiled Bitch.
Clever Girl – BlueStocking; SmartAss; Miss Ingenious; Sensible Sue.

Good Mother – Teacher; Martyr; Soccer Mom; Smother Mother.
Wild Woman – Dancing Queen; SuperModel; Artist; Wicked Stepmother.

Grandam – Gardener; Quilt-Maker; Storyteller; Therapist.
Witch – Evil Hag; Canny Crone; Prophetess; Writer.

Noble Youth – Infant Prince; Child Prodigy; Golden Boy; Hippy.
Urchin – Pickpocket; Barefoot Boy; Hungry Child; Little Brat.

Hero(ine) – Athlete; Activist; Soldier; Volunteer.
Trickster – Villain; Gambler; Rebel; Entrepreneur.

Wise One – Professor; Doctor; Priest; Guru.
Ogre – Tramp; Bully; Fanatic; Foreigner.

Character Worksheet

Full Name:

Known as:

Archetypal role(s):

Birth date & place:

Appearance (hair, eyes, height):

Distinguishing characteristics:

Clothes s/he usually wears:

Personality (5 words):

Flaw or weakness:

Where s/he grew up:

School and/or college:

Skills / Occupation:

Family background:

Love interests:

Children or protégées:

Close personal friends:

Pets (now / childhood):

Talents + Interests:

Favourite colour:

Favourite food:

Favourite music:

Family customs:

Political views:

Religious beliefs:

Proudest of:

Ashamed of:

Eccentric habits:

Catchphrase or
favourite saying:

Other notes:

Business Applications of Stories

Here are some suggestions for stories you could use to convey a message or illustrate a point. You will doubtless be able to think of many others!

What is the ethos of this company? – Fox and Crow (Trickster)

Know your market – Value for Money (Witch)

Benefits of cooperation – Lifting the Sky (Hero)

The value of negotiation – The Bear's Bride (Clever Girl)

Teams can achieve more than individuals – Stone Soup (Stories for Sharing)

Don't judge on first appearances – They Walk Among Us (Ogre)

Take responsibility for your own performance – Blame It On Adam (Noble Youth)

All the parts of your company are important – Hiawatha the Unifier (Wise One)

Don't neglect your original customer base – Poor Turkey Girl (Princess)

You just have to be better than your competitors – Jungle Safaris (Trickster)

Create consumer goodwill at no cost to yourself – Perfect World (Wise One)

Appreciate the basics – Love You Like Salt (Clever Girl)

Seize every opportunity – Perspectives / Carpe Potum (Trickster)

Political embarrassment, surviving scandal – Tar Dolly (Trickster)

Working with your competitors – King of the Birds (Urchin)

Don't automatically follow market trends – Weather Vane (Wise One)

Ethnic diversity in the workplace – Children of the World (Good Mother)

Equality and diversity in the workforce – Safe and Sound (Clever Girl)

Always settle your balance sheet – The Rats of Hamlyn (Ogre)

Don't underestimate your in-house resources – The Frog Bride (Wild Woman)

What price would you be willing to pay? – Tom Saves Becky (Hero)

Maybe there's an easier way – All Crazy Now (Grandam)

Benefits of innovation – The Gordian Knot (Noble Youth)

Slow and steady often wins the race – Sharpen the Axe (Hero)

Marketing is storytelling - Vice Versa (Urchin)

Note: Many stories are universal, but there are variations between cultures which affect how people from different countries behave. People with contrasting stories in their mental repertoire will react very differently in similar situations. In Australia, they say, "The tallest poppy gets cut first." With this moral message, Australians tend to be democratic and egalitarian. In China, "The loudest duck gets shot." Consequently Chinese people value courtesy over confrontation as a way of resolving differences. But in the USA, "The squeaky wheel gets the oil." Americans abroad may think they are acting assertively, when in fact they are violating local social codes. People hear such sayings as children and internalize them, which influences how they behave. In our modern multi-cultural community, it is important to understand that others may be telling different tales. This awareness of diversity will make your stories much more effective.

Bibliography

The stories in the book have reached me in many ways. Some I have been told, and some I have overheard. Some I have read in books; some I have known for so long that I cannot remember where they came from.

The books listed below are some of the many sources of inspiration and insight that have contributed to this collection.

Bain, Jane Bailey. *LifeWorks: Using Myth and Archetype to Develop Your Life Story*. O-Books, Winchester, UK (2012)

Campbell, Joseph. *The Hero With A Thousand Faces*. Princeton University Press, NJ (1949)

Erdoes, Richard & Ortiz, Alfonso. *American Indian Myths and Legends*. Pantheon Books, New York (1984)

Erikson, Milton & Rosen, Sidney (ed). *My Voice Will Go With You*. WW Norton, London, UK (1991)

Gottschall, Jonathan. *The Storytelling Animal*. Houghton Mifflin Harcourt, New York (2012)

Haviland, Virginia. *North American Legends*. Faber & Faber, London, UK (1979)

Mbitu, Ngangar & Prime, Ranchor. *Essential African Mythology*. Thorsons, UK (1997)

Narayan, Kirin. *Mondays on the Dark Night of the Moon*. Oxford University Press (1997)

Owen, Nick. *The Magic of Metaphor*. Crown House Publishing, Carmarthen, UK (2001)

Palma, Ricardo. *Peruvian Traditions*. Oxford University Press (2004)

Te Lin. *Chinese Myths*. Hodder & Stoughton, London, UK (2001)

Yorke, John. *Into the Woods*. Penguin Books, London, UK (2013)

About the Author

Jane Bailey Bain is an author, speaker and executive coach. She studied Psychology at Oxford University and Anthropology at the London School of Economics. Jane trained as a consultant with IBM and worked for several years as an advisor on development projects in Asia and Africa. During this time she became interested in stories and how people use them in everyday life. Jane has lived and travelled around the world including time in America and Australia. She runs courses on Speaking, Writing, Story Structure and Presentation Skills in West London. Her book *LifeWorks* was published in 2012.

.

LifeWorks is a practical handbook which combines insights from psychology and anthropology. It looks at how you compose your 'life script' – the story which you tell about your own life. This script influences how you behave and how you present yourself to other people. *LifeWorks* introduces the twelve major archetypal figures with examples from books and films. Stories and exercises help you to identify people and relationship patterns in your own script. These tools can also be used by writers for character development and plot analysis.

LifeWorks: Using Myth and Archetype to Develop Your Life Story.
O-Books (2012) ISBN 978-1-78099-038-5

**BUSINESS
BOOKS**

Business Books encapsulates the freshest thinkers and the most
successful practitioners in the areas of marketing, management,
economics, finance and accounting, sustainable and ethical
business, heart business, people management, leadership,
motivation, biographies, business recovery and development
and personal/executive development.